VATICAN II IN PLAIN ENGLISH

The
Decrees and
Declarations

VATICAN II IN PLAIN ENGLISH

The
Decrees and
Declarations

by Bill Huebsch

ave maria press AMP notre dame, in

NIHIL OBSTAT
Rev. Msgr. Glenn D. Gardner, J.C.D.
Censor Librorum
IMPRIMATUR
† Most Rev. Charles V. Grahmann
Bishop of Dallas
November 21, 1996

The Nihil Obstat and Imprimatur are official declarations that the material reviewed is free of doctrinal or moral error. No implication is contained therein that those granting the Nihil Obstat and Imprimatur agree with the contents, opinions, or statements expressed.

ACKNOWLEDGMENT

Scripture quotations are adapted from the New Revised Standard Version of the Bible, copyright 1989 by the Division of Christian Education of the National Council of the Churches of Christ in the USA. Used by permission. All rights reserved.

Founded in 1865, Ave Maria Press is a ministry of the Indiana Province of Holy Cross.

www.avemariapress.com

Printed in the United States of America

	ISBN-10	ISBN-13
Book One	1-59471-105-4	978-1-59471-105-3
Book Two	1-59471-106-2	978-1-59471-106-0
Book Three	1-59471-107-0	978-1-59471-107-7
Three Book Set	1-59471-108-9	978-1-59471-108-4

CONTENTS

Introduction
PAGE 11

Chapter One
The Decree on the Apostolate of the Laity
PART ONE: BACKGROUND
PAGE 17
PART TWO: PARAPHRASE TEXT
PAGE 19

Chapter Two
The Decree on Ecumenism
PART ONE: BACKGROUND
PAGE 41
PART TWO: PARAPHRASE TEXT
PAGE 42

Chapter Three
The Declaration on Religious Freedom
PART ONE: BACKGROUND
PAGE 69
PART TWO: PARAPHRASE TEXT
PAGE 71

Chapter Four
*The Declaration on the Relationship
of the Church to Non-Christian Religions*

PART ONE: BACKGROUND
PAGE 85
PART TWO: PARAPHRASE TEXT
PAGE 86

Chapter Five
The Decree on Eastern Catholic Churches
PART ONE: BACKGROUND
PAGE 95
PART TWO: PARAPHRASE TEXT
PAGE 96

Chapter Six
The Decree on the Bishops' Pastoral Office in the Church
PART ONE: BACKGROUND
PAGE 105
PART TWO: PARAPHRASE TEXT
PAGE 107

Chapter Seven
The Decree on the Ministry and Life of Priests
PART ONE: BACKGROUND
PAGE 125
PART TWO: PARAPHRASE TEXT
PAGE 127

Chapter Eight
The Decree on Priestly Formation
PART ONE: BACKGROUND
PAGE 145

PART TWO: PARAPHRASE TEXT
PAGE 146

Chapter Nine
*The Decree on the Appropriate Renewal
of Religious Life*
PART ONE: BACKGROUND
PAGE 159
PART TWO: PARAPHRASE TEXT
PAGE 161

Chapter Ten
*The Decree on the Church's
Missionary Activity*
PART ONE: BACKGROUND
PAGE 173
PART TWO: PARAPHRASE TEXT
PAGE 174

Chapter Eleven
The Declaration on Christian Education
PART ONE: BACKGROUND
PAGE 195
PART TWO: PARAPHRASE TEXT
PAGE 196

Chapter Twelve
*The Decree on the Instruments
of Social Communication*
PART ONE: BACKGROUND
PAGE 205

PART TWO: PARAPHRASE TEXT
PAGE 206

Appendix One
A Brief Summary of the Documents
of Vatican II

PART ONE: THE FOUR CONSTITUTIONS
PAGE 213
PART TWO: THE NINE DECREES
PAGE 218
PART THREE: THE THREE DECLARATIONS
PAGE 224

Appendix Two
A Carefully Annotated Reading List
on Vatican II

PART ONE: THE DOCUMENTS
PAGE 227
PART TWO: GENERAL WORKS ON THE COUNCIL
PAGE 228

Index
PAGE 233

This book is dedicated
to the memory of
Cardinal Leon Josef Suenens

Introduction

*A*s in book two of this series, which presents the four constitutions in plain language and a paraphrased format, here we have the twelve other documents from Vatican II.

Often when these documents are discussed, their Latin titles are used rather than their English ones. This is useful in international dialogue because it provides all participants with the same names, rather than names derived from local translations. The Latin title is taken from the opening two words of each document in its Latin presentation.

For the benefit of readers, here is a list of the Latin names of the documents contained in this volume:

Decrees

On the Instruments of Social Communication
    Inter Mirifica
On Ecumenism
    Unitatis Redintegratio
On Eastern Catholic Churches
    Orientalium Ecclesiarum
On the Bishops' Pastoral Office in the Church
    Christus Dominus
On Priestly Formation
    Optatam Totius
On the Appropriate Renewal of Religious Life
    Perfectae Caritatis
On the Apostolate of the Laity
    Apostolicam Actuositatem

On the Ministry and Life of Priests
   Presbyterorum Ordinis
On the Church's Missionary Activity
   Ad Gentes

Declarations

On Christian Education
   Gravissimum Educationis
On the Relationship of the Church
to Non-Christian Religions
   Nostra Aetate
On Religious Freedom
   Dignitatis Humanae

Format

As with the constitutions in book two, I have chosen to present these paraphrases in sense lines to make them more readable for the average user. Written this way, the documents resemble other spiritual writings and can more easily be used for prayer and reflection. Using sense lines is meant to stimulate midrash, a method of coming to grips with and internalizing spiritual writing. Midrash asks readers to consider the texts thoroughly and then offer their own reflection on them. In so doing, one "owns" the texts and finds one's own words to explain them to others.

Paul Thurmes, another theologian, worked closely with me in preparing one of the documents in this volume. Throughout our work, we retained the article numbers as they appear in the original texts. Sometimes, however, to make the material flow well we reorganized certain articles or borrowed from one article to add a complement to another. A reader should, however, be able to return to a place in any properly numbered text of the originals that corresponds exactly to our numbering.

We were also as faithful to the text as we could be, our own biases aside.

All in all, I see this presentation of the documents of Vatican II as a way for more Catholics, Jews, other Christians, and all people of goodwill, to come to understand the writings of the Second Vatican Council and, having understood them better, to join the worldwide campaign to implement them fully and in so doing to help establish human solidarity and divine presence in our day.

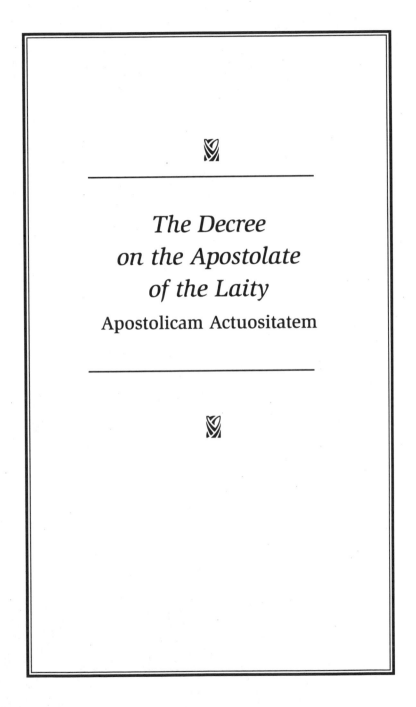

The Decree
on the Apostolate
of the Laity
Apostolicam Actuositatem

Chapter One

⁂

PART ONE: BACKGROUND

*O*ne thing became clear during the Second Vatican Council: laypeople, together with the clergy, bear co-responsibility for the work of the Church, its renewal, and its future. Despite nearly two thousand years of "lay participation" in the ministry of the Church, it was not until this council in the mid-twentieth century that this role was examined, affirmed, and expanded.

Like a race car that moves from zero to sixty miles per hour in a matter of seconds, the laity of the Church moved from their place of mere observation in the pews before the council, to one of vigorous activity in the Church's life and Liturgy after it.

Every single council document discussed the role and place of the laity. The view of the Church put forth in the *Dogmatic Constitution on the Church* addresses the laity directly and includes a chapter explicitly on laypeople. Its chapter on the People of God also directs itself, in part, to a deeper understanding of lay church members.

The *Pastoral Constitution on the Church in the Modern World* also addresses itself to the role of the layperson in the mission of the Church. And many other documents, either directly or indirectly, also do the same.

This should be no surprise. The majority of the members of the Church, after all, are laypeople.

But the document that had the most influence in reforming the place of laypeople in the Church must certainly be the *Constitution on the Sacred Liturgy*. Why? Because once people put away their missals and rosaries during Mass and started actually praying the Liturgy through a more active and full participation in the rites, everything changed for them. The document on the Liturgy speaks of the Eucharist and the Liturgy of the Word as the "source and summit" of the Christian life and rightly so. It also proved to be the source and summit of the renewal of the laity in the Church following the council.

The document on the laity, then, takes its place among the many that address laypeople. The original version of this document was drafted as an effort to give a somewhat full treatment of the role and theology of laypeople in the Church.

Before the schema was even presented for debate, however, large sections of the treatment regarding laypeople were removed and placed in other documents, lacing the treatment of the laity throughout the council's work just as laypeople are laced throughout the Church. (One gets the impression that as the council fathers worked, the realization dawned on them that in speaking of laypeople, they were speaking of the Church, period.)

The gap between lay and clerical roles in the Church, therefore, narrowed significantly because of the council's work.

The version of the document accepted for debate was presented in October 1964 (during the third session), while the council was in its "October Crisis" and very busy debating other key matters. Many found the schema clerical in tone, condescending toward laypeople, and ungrounded in a theology of baptism. Moreover, until the very last minute, no laypeople, despite their presence at the council, had been consulted on the document.

In a speech about the schema, Bishop Carter of Canada said that the document was "conceived in the sin of clericalism." Other speakers likewise called for its revision. Finally, Cardinal Suenens, speaking definitively for the majority, called for it to be reworked before debate would even proceed.

The schema was then sent back to its commission for revisions based on input from the council fathers. It appeared again in the fourth session, when the council fathers approved the document and sent it to the pope. The final vote ran 2,305 to 2. The pope promulgated the *Decree on the Apostolate of the Laity* on November 18, 1965.

PART TWO: PARAPHRASE TEXT

*F*rom the Vatican II document
promulgated on November 18, 1965

Introduction

1 We have already spoken of the important role
of the laity in the constitution on the Church,
but now we wish to expand on that here
because the laity are so essential!
In our day and age,
the laity are needed as never before,
and the Church would scarcely be present
in certain places
without them.

People today face many new challenges
    which are mainly under the leadership
    of laypeople, men and women:
        the expansion of population,
        scientific advancement,
        and technical progress.
We wish, therefore, to offer a description
    of the lay apostolate here
    and to comment on its diversity and theology.
When canon law is revised,
    the norms and principles set forth here
    should be used as its basis.

Chapter One
THE LAYPERSON'S CALL TO THE APOSTOLATE

2 Laypeople are the leaven of the world!
Christians have one goal:
    to spread the word about Christ
    so that all people
    might share in his redemption
        and be brought into relationship
        with God.
The "apostolate" is defined as all activity
    directed to the attainment of that goal.
And all members of the Body of Christ—
    lay, religious, or ordained—
    share in that apostolate.
Every single member of the Body has a role,
    each according to his or her place,
    and fulfilling it is very important
        both to that person

and to the Church itself.
So the laity, like the ordained,
    share in the priestly, or prayerful;
        prophetic, or teaching;
        and royal, or servant, office of Christ.
Their temporal activity,
    when animated by the Spirit of Christ,
    promotes the salvation of all people.

3 Here is the key point:
    the laity derive their right and duty
    to work in this apostolate
        directly from Christ himself,
        not from the Church or its clergy.
Through baptism and confirmation,
    laypeople receive the Holy Spirit
    and are consecrated into that royal priesthood,
        that holy people,
        which is Christ's own.
The sacraments nourish that call
    and provide that grace
    which is the very soul of the apostolate.
The Holy Spirit gives each baptized person gifts
    which, when used properly,
    build up the Body of Christ.
Believers must have the freedom to accept these gifts,
    while at the same time
    they must also cooperate with each other,
    especially their pastors,
        to allow holy order to prevail
        where chaos would otherwise reign.

4 Precisely because Christ is the source
    of the call to ministry and service in the apostolate,

laypeople must live in union with him.
Spiritual aids assist in this,
    especially the sacred Liturgy.
The lay life is to be lived both in Christ
    and in the culture and society of the world,
    not disassociating one from the other.
Everything—family, business concerns, and social lives—
    are to be incorporated into this.

All of this leads to a life of faith, hope, and charity.

By living in faith,
    Christian people see Christ in all,
    whether neighbors or strangers,
    and make accurate assessments
        about meaning and value in life.
This leads to hope
    because we are free from enslavement to wealth
    and able to choose those riches
        that lead to God's Reign.
We are likewise free to see an end to suffering
    and find meaning in human struggle.
And the pinnacle of the Christian life is charity,
    by which Christians choose to do good to all
        and harm to none.
By living the true spirit of the beatitudes,
    laypeople grow in a true sense of poverty:
    which is neither sumptuousness nor destitution.
They grow in a true sense of humility:
    aware of their gifts
    but not seeking empty honors.
They grow in their sense of justice:
    leaving everything to pursue it with vigor.

Whatever their lifestyle—
    married,
    raising children,
    single,
    or widowed—
and whatever their state in life—
    in good health or not,
    professional or laborer,
    private or social—
    all should live with the virtues of
        honesty,
        justice,
        sincerity,
        kindness,
        and courage.
The Blessed Virgin Mary is the true model of this:
    she lived a common life animated by Christ.

Chapter Two
OBJECTIVES

5 Christ's saving work is intended both
    for all men and women in the Church
    as well as for all aspects of life in the world
        as we live it here and now.
The laity have, therefore, a two-level ministry:
    in the Church itself
    as well as in the everyday world
        in which they live.
Even though these two dimensions of life are distinct,
    they are also intimately joined in God's plan

and Christians, living in them simultaneously,
should be led by their consciences in both.

6 Let us reflect on both aspects of Christ's work.
First, the mission of the Church
    is primarily to communicate God's grace
    to the world through Christ's deeds and words.
This is done mainly through the sacraments,
    entrusted in a special way to the clergy.
By their way of life and their explicit witness,
    laypeople contribute to this as well
    and invite others to join the Church.
We urge laypeople to apply Christian principles
    to more of today's modern human challenges.

7 Second, the mission of the world
    is to be that place
    where people live their "everydayness."
It includes many aspects of life:
    good things and prosperity;
    family, culture, economic life;
    the arts and other professions;
    and politics and international relations.
All of these are divinely created, seen as good,
    and joined with the supernatural,
    giving them great value in fulfilling human destiny.
People have sometimes fallen into error
    regarding the true nature of human life
    and these aspects of the world.
Blinded by sin, people have become selfish
    and unilateral.
Sure that science can save them,
    people have fallen into a modern form of idolatry
    and have become slaves to technology,

rather than its manager.
This is where the Church and the world
    merge and affect one another.
The Church can offer meaning and understanding,
    as well as moral and spiritual aids.
It can, through its lay members,
    restore the world to its created purpose
    and establish God's justice on earth.

8 The basic underlying principle of this Christian message
    to the world is this:
        Love.
Everything Christians do should be motivated by love,
    but certain activities are especially loving:
        pity for the needy,
        care of the sick,
        and other works of charity.
Today the world is reduced to a single family
    in which everyone knows of the needs of others,
    making charity more urgent and extensive.
Christian social action should, therefore,
    reach out to every single person on earth
    who is in need,
      regardless of their faith,
        to offer food and drink;
        clothing, housing, medicine;
        employment, education, and freedom.
Christians should seek those in need,
    search for and find them wherever they are,
    and offer them solace and comfort.
This duty is enjoined on every person
    and wealthy nation in the world!
And here are key principles to follow in this ministry:
    Pay attention to the image of God

in the ones who are needy.
Preserve their freedom and dignity
even as they are fed and clothed.
Maintain pure motive as the helper:
not to dominate but to serve.
The demands of justice are to be met first,
thus alleviating the need for future charity
by eliminating the root causes
of the poverty or pain.
Cooperation among those who can help,
both publicly and privately,
will serve all best.

Chapter Three
THE VARIOUS FIELDS OF THE APOSTOLATE

⁹ There are various ways in which the laity
carry out their apostolic work,
and we wish to mention each of them.
We also wish to point out that women
have an ever increasing role in this,
and it is important that they be encouraged
in all of the Church's work.
¹⁰ First, the parish is an obvious place
where laypeople work in the apostolate,
exercising their priestly, or prayerful;
prophetic, or teaching;
and royal, or servant, share in ministry.
Taking their strength from the Eucharist,
laypeople assist in making the parish
a place where everyone can be spiritually fed.
They invite people to the Church,

teach those who are there,
    use their skills to care for souls,
    and administer the materialities of the parish.
In this, laypeople should work in close union
    with their pastors,
        bringing today's human dilemmas to the table
            and earnestly seeking the truth about them.
They should also move beyond the parish
    to assist the diocesan and national Church as well,
    including missionary work when possible.

11 Second, God created sexual intercourse
    as the beginning and basis of human relationships
    and filled it with grace,
        making it part of the mystery of the Church.
Therefore, marriage and family life
    is another obvious place where laypeople
    live out their apostolate as Christian ministers.
The home is where faith begins for children.
It is where fidelity is experienced
    and love developed.
Christians should do everything possible
    to structure their particular society and culture
    to support stable and holy family life
        through legislation;
        housing, education, and welfare;
        social security and the tax system;
        and assistance to migrants
            who often travel as families.
The household is the domestic sanctuary of the Church
    where common prayer,
    shared liturgical life,
    and active hospitality are the lifestyle.
Families and households can provide the world with

adoption of abandoned infants,
hospitality for strangers and travelers,
help to operate schools,
advice and support for young people,
preparation for those to be married,
the teaching of religion,
support for other married couples,
care for those in crisis,
and assistance to the aged.

12 Third, another obvious place where the apostolate works
is among young people.
Young folks are challenged today
by fast-moving modern lifestyles
and some appear unable to cope well.
But youthful energy and fresh ideas abound here,
and young people can minister to each other
and help the whole Church.
A strong and vital relationship should exist
between youth and adults,
providing both with benefits.

13 Fourth, the social lives of Christians
provide yet another opportunity
to develop the apostolate.
This is done by infusing and animating the world
with the spirit of Christ
in the workplace,
university and college,
home life,
recreation and leisure life,
and among our companions.
If Christians live lives that are in harmony
with the values of the Gospel—

honesty,
charity,
and fidelity—
    others will see them
    and be affected.
Little by little through their lifestyles,
    Christians will penetrate the world
    and announce the Gospel.

14 And fifth, by promoting the common good
    on a national and international level,
    Christians touch the whole world.
Those with the skills and desire for this work
    should not hesitate to become public leaders
    so that they can prepare the way of the Gospel
        through their efforts.
Christians should support social research
    and promote the common good
    whenever possible.
We applaud the increasing sense of solidarity
    among people of the world
    and hope it will become genuine love.
Wherever they go, Christians announce Christ
    by their lives and witness.

Chapter Four
THE VARIOUS METHODS OF THE APOSTOLATE

15 Laypeople come to their work
    in building the Reign of God
    either as individuals or as groups.
16 Let us consider both ways.

There is no substitute for the individual ministry
    that people undertake,
    and in fact, such individual work
        underpins group work as well.
Everyone is called to this kind of ministry,
    and sometimes individual work is all that is possible.
First, the most dramatic and powerful form
    of the individual apostolate
    is the witness of a Christian person's very life!
Second, and following on that as a form of ministry,
    is the occasion when a person
    explicitly announces and explains
        his or her faith in Christ.
Third, these two forms—
    a holy lifestyle coupled with a clear witness—
    lead to collaboration of Christians with others
    in building up the everyday world
        as a place of value.
And fourth, laypeople animate their lives
    through public prayer and penance
    as well as through Christian charity and love,
        the highest virtue.
[17] There is an urgent need for individual ministry
    in places where the preaching of the Gospel
    is prohibited or restricted,
        often resulting in heroic efforts
        to witness and minister to others.
This is also true in places where Catholics are few
    and where they live far from one another,
        for in these places no organized program
        of Christian sharing may exist
        and people may feel unusually isolated.
[18] Group ministry, on the other hand,
    gives powerful witness to the Body of Christ

and also expresses a great human need
> to gather as community.
Laypeople exercise an important ministry
> in their families,
> in their parishes,
> in their dioceses,
> and in other voluntary groups they join.
Such group ministry sustains the members
> and serves the Gospel extremely well.
We want to see lay ministry strengthened today
> so that by staying close to one another,
> the faithful might remain strong.

19 Among the many organized apostolates today,
> the most effective are those
> that harmonize everyday life and everyday faith.
The point here is that organizing as such
> is not our goal!
Infusing the world and everyday living
> with the Spirit of Christ is our goal,
> and we organize to get that done.

Therefore, any organized effort must have that mission
> in mind or it is not valid.
We would also like to see greater effort to organize
> Catholic ministry on a group basis
> in the international sphere.
Catholics have the right to organize like this
> on various levels of apostolic work
> provided they have a proper relationship
> > to church authorities.

20 This council endorses that form of apostolic work
> which has emerged over the years

and has been called "Catholic Action."
Here is how we define Catholic Action:
    The group's aim is the same as that of the Church
        as a whole.
    The laity assume leadership
        in cooperation with the hierarchy
        and carry out a program of action.
    The laity involved act as a body.
    And the laity function under the authority
        of church hierarchy.
21 We especially endorse those organizations
    that have been recommended
    by various bishops.
22 And we are very pleased with those laypeople
    who have dedicated their entire lives
    to this work.

Chapter Five
THE PRESERVATION OF GOOD ORDER

23 A necessary feature of the lay apostolate,
    whether individual or group,
    is its link to the whole Church
    and the right relationships that define it.
This means that all lay activity
    should be ordered and coordinated
    by the hierarchy under the guidance
        of the Holy Spirit.
This will prevent chaos from overtaking us
    and allow for the pursuit of common goals
    and the avoidance of destructive competition.
And this will bring all ministers—

lay, religious, and ordained—
    into harmony with one another.
24 For their part, the hierarchy should promote
    the work of the laity
    by providing it with spiritual leadership,
        support,
        and direction.
While laypeople have the right to organize
    or undertake apostolic work individually,
    no one may use the name "Catholic"
    without the consent of church authority.
The hierarchy may, if it chooses,
    select and promote certain apostolates
    because of their benefit to the Church,
    but this does not preclude laypeople
        from acting on their own accord as well.
Certain pastoral activities,
    such as teaching,
    caring for souls,
    and some liturgical functions,
        can also be entrusted to laypeople
        while remaining fully subject
        to ecclesiastical direction.
The hierarchy even has the right to rule and judge
    after consideration of all features of it,
    regarding affairs outside the Church
        in the "temporal order."
25 Bishops and pastors are to work closely with laypeople
    in building up the Church.
In particular, priests should be carefully chosen
    who are willing and able to promote lay ministry
    and nourish those who step forward.
Through ongoing dialogue and consultation,
    priests should be on the lookout for new forms

of fruitful apostolic work.
Religious men and women, for their part,
    should also support lay ministry
    as well as that of the ordained.

26 Overall, we are saying that lay ministry
    is to be encouraged,
        supported,
        and carefully coordinated.
Toward this end,
    dioceses should establish councils
    through which apostolic work and ministry
    can be fostered and coordinated.
Such councils should exist at all levels of the Church:
    within parishes,
    among parishes,
    among dioceses,
    and among nations.
Also toward this end,
    a special office should be established in Rome
    staffed by representatives of various apostolates
        to serve and encourage lay ministry.
27 Also toward this end,
    programs of cooperation should be fostered
    among various Christian Churches
        as well as among other good people
        who share the values of the Gospel
        if not belief in Jesus Christ.

Chapter Six
FORMATION FOR THE APOSTOLATE

28 Laypeople who take up ministerial work
   should be well trained and prepared
   both in understanding doctrine
   and in adapting to the needs
      of the particular circumstance
      in which they are working.
Such formation should be based on fundamentals
   outlined in the *Dogmatic Constitution on the Church*
   and the *Decree on Ecumenism*
   in addition to training specific to their tasks.
29 Preparation for lay ministry
   emerges and is formed by the distinctive quality
   of being a layperson and having a lay spirituality.
This means a layperson should take up work
   reflecting his or her natural talents.
Above all, a lay minister advances the Gospel
   by living out belief in the divine mysteries,
   by sensing the movement of the Holy Spirit,
   and by moving ever closer to God.
Beyond this spiritual reality,
   lay ministers also need training in theology,
      ethics,
      philosophy,
      technical skills,
      human relations,
      and cultural realities.
They should be given opportunities for internships
   through which practical knowledge develops.
30 Preparation for lay ministry begins in childhood
   and is continued through youthful experiences
   in the context of family and parish life.

Schools and colleges continue the formation process,
    and where there are no such schools,
    other institutes should be established to do this.
In adulthood, lay groups and associations
    take up the task of training as well,
    providing doctrinal, spiritual, and practical formation.
Here members meet in small groups
    to appraise their Christian lives
    and evaluate their ministry.
Everyone should, therefore,
    painstakingly ready himself or herself
    for apostolic work in adulthood,
        because as we grow older
            we can contribute more.
[31] Certain forms of the apostolate demand greater training.
First, for those engaged in announcing the Gospel
    and leading others to holiness,
    ministers must be formed in human relations
    and the ability to articulate doctrine clearly.
Second, for those working in the everyday world,
    ministers should be trained in ethics,
    organizational development,
        and social doctrine.
Third, for those engaged in works of charity and mercy,
    attention should be paid to the development
        of compassion.
[32] There already exists a vast array of resources
    for the training of lay ministers,
    including academic and formation institutes,
        and we applaud this.
We call for even more
    and for centers in which the study of theology
    can be expanded to include
        anthropology,

psychology,
sociology,
and methodology,
    all for the better development
    of lay ministry.

Exhortation

33 We urge all laypeople
    who are moved by the Holy Spirit
    to gladly and promptly accept their calling
        to minister in the Church and the world.
This calling comes, after all,
    from God through Christ
    so that we might move closer to the divine heart
        and prepare the way of the Lord!

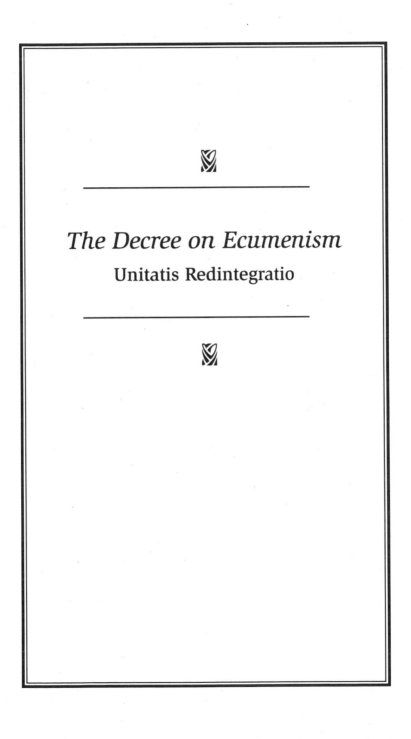

The Decree on Ecumenism

Unitatis Redintegratio

Chapter Two

⁂

PART ONE: BACKGROUND

*T*here may not have been a more consistent theme at Vatican II than the one this document takes up explicitly. From the beginning to the end of Vatican II, sensitivity to ecumenical dialogue was taken into account as the council fathers enacted reform.

Before the council began, Pope John XXIII had made clear that the restoration of unity was a primary goal of the council and of his pontificate. And indeed, in the first major council discussion, which was on the Liturgy, the bishops made clear that they, too, realized that liturgical renewal could have widespread effects in promoting Christian unity.

In the next major debate, which was on the sources of divine revelation, the council rejected an original schema on the matter in part because it would not have encouraged ecumenical dialogue among Christians.

The opening speeches both of Pope John XXIII and of Pope Paul VI as well as the council debates made one goal clear: Vatican II wanted to promote Christian unity. Indeed, many other Christians were seated among the council's guests as honored and respected brothers and sisters.

When Cardinal Bea presented the first draft of this schema to the council, it was received with enthusiasm and gratitude. Not enough can be said about the role of Bea in the development of this movement and this document at the council. He was tireless in his efforts.

At least three council documents, including this one, had profound influence on the matter of ecumenism. The *Declaration on the Relationship of the Church to Non-Christian Religions* and the *Declaration on Religious Freedom* also opened many doors in the ecumenical arena. But the *Decree on Ecumenism* provided an explicit set of principles and encouraged the Church's full participation in the ecumenical movement. The final ceremonial vote was taken on November 21, 1964, and ran 2,137 in favor to 11 opposed.

For the first time since the Reformation in the sixteenth century, the Catholic Church spoke in this document of other Christians in terms other than "heretics and apostates." This document refers to other Christians as "sister and brother Churches." In this document, the Catholic Church admits that the fault for the divisions among Christians is a result of sin on both sides. This decree encourages all to act and to pray, to study and to talk, to plan and coordinate, so that hearts might be changed and the Gospel served more fully.

We have said of many council documents that they opened, not ended, the discussion in the Church and among the Churches. Of none could that better be said than this one.

PART TWO: PARAPHRASE TEXT

*F*rom the Vatican II document
promulgated on November 21, 1964

Introduction

1 To reestablish unity among all Christian people
    is one of the principal intentions
    of this Second Vatican Council.
Christ established one Church
    and only one Church.
However, at the present time
    the Church is not unified;
        it is not "one."
Therefore, we believe it is not
    what Christ intended.
Instead, there are many groups and individuals,
    all of whom claim to be followers of Christ,
        presenting themselves
        as the exclusive way to God.
Yet each has a separate mind and heart,
    and each walks a different path
    as if Christ himself were divided!
This is not a matter to be taken lightly.
Such division blatantly contradicts
    the will of Christ.
Moreover, it gives scandal to the world
    and damages the most fervent cause of Christians,
    which is to present the Good News
        to all of creation.

While our present situation gives us
    much to be concerned about,
    we also see signs that the will of Christ
    is beginning to sink deeply
        into the hearts of humankind.
To us who have sinned by separating ourselves
    from one another,

God still remains faithful,
    moving us along the eternal path
    with wisdom and patience.
Hence, by the grace of the Holy Spirit,
    our divisions have finally begun
    to strike a discordant sound within us.
We recognize this sound
    as one that is out of harmony
        with God's voice.
It is the sound of remorse over our divisions
    and longing for genuine unity.
This heartfelt remorse and longing
    have given rise to a great movement
    whose goal is the restoration of unity
        among all Christians.

This movement is appropriately called *ecumenical*,
    a word which means
    "to inhabit the whole world together."

Those who believe in one God
    and confess that Jesus Christ is Lord and Savior
        know that their faith has the power
        to bring salvation.
Yet believers everywhere still long for something more:
    for all Christians to live together in peace.
We long to live together as one family,
    with the whole world
    as our peaceful dwelling place
        united in one visible Church.
Only then will the truth of the Gospel
    shine forth clearly!
Its light will then be so compelling

that the whole world will be drawn
    to God's gift of salvation.

We who are assembled for this Second Vatican Council
    gladly note the progress toward unity
    that Christians everywhere have made.
We also recognize this movement
    as the grace of God
    and the work of the Holy Spirit.
Having already discussed the nature of the Church
    and its teachings and spirit
    in the document *Lumen Gentium*,
    we now wish to specifically address Catholics
    about our role in the restoration of Christian unity.
In this document, we place before Catholics
    some helps,
    some guidelines,
    and some methods
    by which we can all respond with grace
        to our common vocation
        to foster unity among Christ's disciples.

Chapter One
CATHOLIC PRINCIPLES ON ECUMENISM

2 The goal of Christian unity is fundamentally based
    on the person and mission of Jesus Christ.
The way we actually know of God's eternal love is this:
    that God sent Jesus Christ to live with us,
        to inhabit the same world with us
            as a human being,
            as a member of our family.

Christ offers redemption to all of humankind
    and, in doing so, gives us hope for new life
    and a reason for wholehearted unity.

Jesus longed desperately for such unity.
His last prayer before going to the cross
    was a heartfelt petition
    that the whole human family
        could truly experience holy unity.
"That all will be one," John's Gospel retells this prayer,
    "as you Father are in me and I in you;
        that they will be one in us
        and that the world may believe
            that you sent me." (17:21)
And Christ gave us the means and the strength
    to make this ideal a reality
        rather than just a dream.
He provided us the gifts that become tools
    to construct a unified Church
    for the sake of a unified world.

The gift of the Eucharist is the first we receive:
    the food,
    the strength,
    and the Spirit that makes this unity possible.
The Eucharist is both a sign of unity in the Church
    and the power that brings this unity
    into existence.
Another gift is a new command:
    "Love one another."
No words could be more compelling
    or more difficult to live
        yet none are more full of life-giving
            and unifying potential.

The third gift is a promise:
    "I will send you the Holy Spirit."
The promise of the Holy Spirit
    gives humankind the assurance
    of God's eternal presence
        in this struggle to be united.

Given these gifts
    and their power to transform us,
    it is clear to us that the Church has a role,
        particular and gifted,
        in the task of constructing unity.
Through the Holy Spirit,
    the Church is called to be
        a unity of faith,
        hope,
        and charity.
By baptism, the faithful are joined to this unity
    and are able to experience
    compelling intimacy with Christ.
This intimacy is expressed as a communion,
    a sense of being "at home" with all believers,
    and it is enriched by the gifts of the Holy Spirit—
    gifts of service for all who are called to be saints.
The Church and the Body of Christ
    are built up little by little
    when the faithful enter into loving service
        of their sisters and brothers.

And Christ intended that the Church
    should build itself and spread itself
    to all corners of the earth,
    thus making the benefits of the Gospel
        accessible to all humankind.

Therefore, the twelve apostles,
    under the leadership of Peter,
    were entrusted with the task
        of keeping the whole Church
        united in Christ.
The apostles brought unity to the Church
    by the ministry of teaching,
    by the celebration of the sacraments,
    and by giving leadership to the Church.
In this, they lived out the work of Christ,
    who lives among us as Teacher,
        as One Who Prays,
        and as Servant Ruler.
Today this ministry of unity is still maintained
    in the person of the pope and the bishops,
    who have been entrusted with the work
        of the first apostles.

3 Now let us remind all
    that the struggle for unity which we face today
    is not new to this age.
In fact, in the early days of the Church,
    there arose disputes and controversies
    that threatened the unity of the Church.
At first these differences were manageable.
But as the centuries wore on,
    so, too, did the dissension and obstacles.
Eventually, large Christian communities
    became separated from one another:
    an unfortunate reality for which both sides
        were often at fault.
This council, however, wishes to make clear
    that today the guilt does not lie
    with those who are left to deal

with the consequences
of the sins of their ancestors.
The Catholic Church embraces all Christians
as sisters and brothers.
By baptism, all Christians are formed
in the likeness of Christ
and therefore share in a common union
with the Catholic Church.
This communion is not yet perfect.
Indeed, the differences in doctrine,
discipline,
and structure
create many obstacle to full communion.
Nonetheless, we share together a bond with Christ
that cannot be severed.
The ecumenical movement
seeks to build on this reality
and use what we share in common
as a basis for overcoming all the other obstacles.
We believe that in baptism,
the grace of Christ is offered to all
and that it leads people to the truth,
which is sometimes found outside
the visible boundaries of the Catholic Church.
The baptized, whoever they are,
receive gifts, such as the Word of God;
the gifts of charity,
faith,
hope;
an interior life;
and countless gifts of loving service.

Moreover, the strong religious and liturgical practices
of other churches,

provided they are truly authentic
and guided by the Holy Spirit,
    lead people to Christ.

We believe and proclaim
    that whatever leads people to Christ,
    even if it be outside the Catholic Church,
    rightly belongs to the one Church of Christ.
The separated Churches do have access to salvation,
    and they do play a valid role
    in bringing about salvation on earth.

And even though we believe this,
    we still maintain that the Catholic Church alone
    provides the fullness of the means of salvation.
Salvation is not limited just to Catholics,
    nor, for that matter, just to Christians.
But only the Catholic Church
    has kept every element of the faith intact,
    even if it has not always lived that faith
        as well as it could have.
Only the Catholic Church has kept
    the full apostolic leadership
    that Christ intended
        since the founding of the Church.

4 The work of ecumenism
    is the work of the Holy Spirit.
All over the world, people are engaged
    in prayer, words, and actions
    in order to obtain full Christian unity.
We wish to affirm such efforts on the part of Catholics
    and encourage them to continue their work.
In this ecumenical movement,

specific efforts are being made
    to make this dream of unity
        a reality for the whole Church.
The efforts that individuals and groups are taking
    include five important elements:
First, people are nurturing a sense of truth
    about various denominations
        rather than proceeding with past prejudices
        and false perceptions.
Second, they are joining together in dialogue
    in order to gain a greater appreciation
    of the richness of each denomination.
Third, they are cooperating with one another to address
    the pressing needs of society around them.
Fourth, they are joining together in prayer.
And fifth, they are humbly examining their own religion
    to determine if it is in line with the will of Christ.
        If it is not, they are then making efforts
        for reform where necessary.
These and other actions, when carried out
    under the guidance of the Holy Spirit
    and the leadership of the Church,
        promote justice and truth.
Little by little, this will lead to full Christian unity.

Someday all Christians will gather together
    to celebrate the Eucharist
    as God's one and holy Church.
Such unity can already be found in the Catholic Church,
    and we must make every effort
    to make this unity increase
        until it is full and complete.

While it is important for Catholics to be concerned

about their sisters and brothers in other Churches
and to invite them to know the Catholic Church,
    our primary responsibility as Catholics
    is to make sure that our own household
        is in order.
Only when we confront our own shortcomings
    and make the necessary reforms
    will we truly be able to discern the will of Christ
        and bear witness to Christ's teaching.
Yes, through the grace of God,
    the Catholic Church has maintained
    the truth that was first given to us.
But through shortcomings,
    stubbornness,
    and sin,
        the Catholic Church as a whole
        and the individual members within it
        have often failed to understand this truth
            and to live by it.
Sometimes we have moved away from God's Reign
    rather than moved toward it.
The role of each member, then,
    is to aim at Christian perfection.
All in the Church must try to live freely,
    listening for the voice of the Holy Spirit.
They must give expression to the authentic prompting
    of this Spirit, which will lead all to see
    the true nature of the Catholic Church.
The Catholic Church is unified yet diverse,
    embracing all cultures
    yet true to our apostolic roots.
Catholics seek Christ wherever he can be found
    and gratefully acknowledge the ways
    that other denominations contribute

to our understanding of the Christian mission.
Catholics realize that any action grounded in authentic faith
is for the good of God's one Church.

The separation that the Church is presently experiencing
is more than just an unfortunate situation.
It prevents the Church from fully realizing its true nature
as *catholic*,
a word that means "universal."
It prevents us from truly being one household
of faith living in the family of God.
Therefore, this council once again wishes to commend
those who are involved in the vital work
of ecumenism
and to encourage all to take an active role
in reconciling our differences.

Chapter Two
THE PRACTICE OF ECUMENISM

5 All Catholics, whether laity, religious, or clergy,
are to be involved in the work of restoring unity.
This, of course, is to be done in the context
of one's own life and calling,
using the gifts and talents that God has given
in the most effective and appropriate way.
6 Whenever the Church experiences authentic renewal,
it always consists in increased faithfulness
to its own vocation.
This is why the ecumenical movement is so dynamic.
It is not an "aside" or a movement away
from the "real" work of the Church.

Instead, it is the very heart of the Church's
    true calling and mission.

The fact that over the ages
    the Church has not always been true to this calling
    does not take away from its place
        in the heart of our faith.
Whatever has been a stumbling block to authentic unity
    ought to be set right at the most appropriate time
        and in the most appropriate way.

Already some of these deficiencies are being overcome
    as a result of the ecumenical movement.
Some of the changes that are already happening include:
    a renewed hunger for Scripture,
    great strides in the area of liturgical renewal,
    an increased fervor for meaningful preaching,
    new and more meaningful forms of religious life,
    fuller awareness of the spirituality of married life,
    and increased action to bring about social justice.

7 All truly authentic ecumenism brings about renewal
    in the whole Church and in the individual as well.
Indeed, authentic ecumenism
    must bring about interior conversion.
Those who desire Christian unity
    must always strive to cultivate
    newness of the mind and heart
        and unlimited love.
From such a heart arises a mature desire for unity,
    and such unity is attained
    in the practice of self-sacrifice,
        humble and gentle service,
        and generosity of spirit.

The best way to promote Christian unity
    is to strive for holiness in one's own life.

8 This holiness of life, both through external actions
    and through an internal change of heart,
    along with prayer for Christian unity,
        is really the soul
        of this ecumenical movement.
Prayer services with members of other Christian Churches
    are strongly encouraged.
They are a particularly effective way
    of receiving the grace that we need
    to overcome our hurts and divisions.
Such prayer also expresses a great deal of the unity
    that all Christians share.
However, such prayer should not be used as a "cover-up"
    for the divisions that do, in fact, exist.
Prayer services need to be carefully considered:
    It is important that Christians
    try not to give one another a false sense of unity
        by pretending that differences do not exist.
But prayer is also the most important means
    for us to receive the grace that we need
        to establish full and real unity.
Care should be taken in planning joint prayer services
    that both these values are maintained:
    the need to pray and the need to be honest
        about where we differ.
The local bishop is the one who is best able to judge
    the wisest course of action
    for such relations among separated Christians.

9 Besides prayer and action,
    study is also absolutely necessary

to achieve Christian unity.
It is important that Catholics really try to understand
the history,
the doctrine,
the culture,
the worship,
and the spirituality
of other Christians.
But it is not enough just to read about them.
We must also enter into honest dialogue,
treating each other as equals
and coming to greater clarity
about our actual situations.
We must focus more on the truth
and less on preconceived notions
and biased opinions.

10 Those preparing for leadership in the Church
must approach the study of theology
with an adequate view of ecumenism.
It is especially important that priests
receive adequate formation
in the area of ecumenism
because their training will actually be the basis
for the training of most people in a typical parish.

11 While understanding the views of other Christians
is important,
it is equally important
that Catholic doctrine be fully understood
by Catholics themselves.
We cannot really understand the beliefs of others
until we come to fully understand our own treasure.
When we dig deeply

into the profound teaching of the Church,
we will bring true Catholic teaching
    to light for ourselves and for others.
When we teach about our doctrine,
    we should not do so in a way that presents
    the Catholic faith as "better" than other religions.
Such an approach could itself become an obstacle to unity.
On the other hand, we cannot pretend
    we are something that we are not,
    just for the sake of unity.
We must also remember that in Catholic teaching
    some things are more important than others.
        Not all doctrines and ideas
        carry the same weight.

12 Given all the urgent needs the world is facing today,
    it is the responsibility of all people to work together
    to bring about solutions to the world's problems.
It is even more important that all who believe in God
    find a way to cooperate in a spirit of goodness
    and work together for a better world.
And in this regard, Christians have no choice.
If we believe in Christ's love,
    then all who are Christian must work together
    to make that love a concrete reality for humanity.
It is really that simple.

We must work together to banish from the earth
    all poverty,
    injustice,
    illiteracy,
    lack of housing,
    and unequal distribution of wealth.
Hence, by working together, all Christians will discover

that the task of Christian unity
is really quite simple:
It is about revealing Christ's love on earth.

Chapter Three
CHURCHES AND CHURCH COMMUNITIES
SEPARATED FROM THE ROMAN CATHOLIC CHURCH

13 Having spoken about
the general state of ecumenism in the Church
and the general practice of ecumenism,
we now wish to deal specifically with
two distinct divisions
that run through the Christian community.

The first division is between the Roman Catholic Church
and the Eastern Churches.
Historically, this division is quite long-standing,
having developed during the first thousand years
of church history.
The second division is newer
but in some ways more serious
because of the questions around which it arose.
This division is a result of the events of the Reformation.
The Churches that were formed as a result of this event
in the sixteenth century
are often referred to as Protestant.

The Eastern Catholic Churches

14 We begin by considering the relationship between
the Roman Catholic Church
and the Eastern Churches.

For many years there have existed divisions
    between these two bodies,
      but for the most part these divisions
        were not the result of anger or disputes.
Instead, these differences arose from differences in culture
    and in practices of worship.
Questions and disputes were generally referred to Rome,
    which acted as a sort of moderator,
      seeking consensus
      among the various Churches.

A little bit of history:
In the West, the Church has always depended
    on one governing body, which held authority
      over all other church bodies.
Hence, today, every diocese of the Roman Catholic Church
    in every part of the world looks to Rome
      for leadership,
      guidance,
      and ultimate decision-making authority.
The Eastern Churches, however, are not characterized
    by this form of leadership.
Instead, the Eastern Churches considered Rome to be
    one important Church among several equals.
They also looked to the Patriarchal Churches
    (which are in those areas where the Church
    was established by apostles other than Peter),
    as well as to other local Churches,
      for cooperation.

The Churches of the East have strong and vibrant traditions
    of Liturgy, spirituality, and teaching,
    which contribute a great deal to the whole Church.
These traditions are a result of the faith being handed on
    to different cultures with varying mentalities.

Faith and the practice of faith being so rooted in culture,
     it makes sense that such differences would arise.
Such differences are to be considered
     as gifts of the Holy Spirit.
However, the actual divisions
     that came as a result of these practices
     are not due to legitimate differences of expression,
     but to a lack of charity and understanding
          on both sides.
In the work of ecumenism, then,
     it is important to recognize
     that most of our differences are the result
     of legitimate differences in expression
          of the same faith.
We need to resolve our hostilities,
     not end our differences.

15 Let us consider now in detail
     some of the unique contributions
     that the Eastern Churches have brought to
          to the Church as a whole.
In the celebration of Liturgy, especially the Eucharist,
     the East has a beautiful and profound love
          for the mystery of faith.
In the celebration of the Eucharist,
     where we in the West have focused
     on the real presence of Christ,
     the East has been more mindful
          of the real presence of the Trinity.
What a gift it is to remind the whole Church
     that through the Eucharist,
     we share in the deep and intimate relationship
          of the three persons of the Trinity!

There has also been in the East a long tradition
    of rich liturgical and doctrinal development
    that honors Mary as the Mother of God
       and gives great respect to the other saints.
The spiritual life of the Eastern Churches has been
    and continues to be quite profound.
From the East arose the monastic tradition
    and the development of divine contemplation,
    which has had a profound effect on the whole Church.
Perhaps the most important factor
    in the ecumenical dialogue
    is the fact that the Eastern Churches
    and the Roman Catholic Church mutually recognize
       that the other possesses true sacraments,
       especially Eucharist and priesthood.
Therefore, common worship in appropriate circumstances
    is to be promoted and highly encouraged.

16 As we have already acknowledged,
    the Churches of the East
    have always had traditions and forms of leadership
       that differ from those in the West.
These differences are to be seen not as obstacles to unity,
    but as holy and beautiful expressions of diversity.
At this council we solemnly declare
    that the Eastern Churches have the right and duty
    to govern themselves and their own practices.
Those whose heritage is this tradition are best qualified
    to make decisions about their particular Churches.
The unity of East and West rests upon the recognition
    that the East holds authority in matters that pertain
       to its own discipline and traditions.

17 With regard to doctrinal truths,
    this council also affirms that differences
    in the expression of such truths
        are to be highly valued.
Rather than being opposed to each other,
    such expressions actually complement one another.
Neither the East nor the West is "missing" something,
    but together, both give a fuller picture of
        what our faith is really all about.
Such complementarity allows
    for a more complete expression of the truth
    which belongs to the whole Church.
These differences, put together,
    are actually an essential element
    in making the whole Church
        both "catholic" and "apostolic."

18 In restoring unity between Rome and the Eastern Churches,
    this council affirms
    what has been stated in previous proclamations:
        "Impose no burdens
        beyond what is indispensable."
In other words, the East and the West
    should not make unnecessary demands
    and unreasonable requests of each other.
The expectations that we place on each other
    should be only those that are essential
    to maintaining the integrity
    of the respective Churches.

Both parties can, over time and with mutual understanding,
    let go of those expectations
    that simply are not essential to the faith.
Such recognition of the essential and the nonessential

will allow all to see more clearly
    and experience more profoundly
    the faith that the whole Church possesses.
In this way, true and lasting unity
    between East and West can be firmly established,
    and together, we can truly dwell as one family,
    sharing this one world as our home.

The Separated Churches and Church Communities in the West

19 All Christians share a common bond
    of hope for things to come
    and faith in Jesus Christ,
        who promises eternal life.
Those Churches that were separated
    from the Catholic Church
    during the Middle Ages and into the Reformation
        have an additional bond
        with the Catholic Church.
Having shared centuries of common heritage and faith,
    these Churches continue to have
        a special relationship
        with the Catholic Church.

There is, however, a major difficulty here.
Since Protestant Churches differ
    not only from the Catholic Church
    but also from each other,
    it is nearly impossible to describe our relationships
        in a single document such as this.
Therefore, this council does not attempt here
    to make such a description.

While we rejoice that within many church communities
    there is a genuine desire to restore unity
    with their Catholic brothers and sisters,
    we acknowledge that this ecumenical desire
        is not present in all the Churches.
We also recognize that although there are many similarities
    between the Catholic Church and other Churches,
    there are many aspects
    that remain as stumbling blocks to full unity.
Without ignoring these differences,
    we wish to outline those aspects
    that can serve as a basis for further dialogue
        and closer unity.
20 The first aspect, of course, is our common belief
    in the one and only one God, who is revealed
        in Jesus Christ as Lord and Savior.
And while we may describe this belief in varying terms
    and may understand this reality differently,
    nevertheless, this belief is still our foundation.
Such faith is a powerful starting point for full communion.

21 Scripture is another element upon which
    there is hope of establishing fuller unity.
While other Churches may understand Scripture
    in a different way than Catholics do,
    these communities still have cultivated
    a particularly strong reverence for sacred Scripture.
In our mutual dialogue, let us use the grace
    that comes to us through the Word of God
    to bring about the unity that Christ desires.

22 Baptism is also a gift
    that most Christian Churches share.
By baptism, we are incorporated

into the death and resurrection of Jesus Christ
    and gain access to divine eternal life.
Baptism is a beginning, not an end,
    of sharing in Christian life.
Baptism as a full sharing in Christian life
    is ultimately directed toward Eucharist.
We cannot recognize as sacramental
    the eucharistic celebrations of those communities
    that have not preserved priesthood.
Nonetheless, their celebrations of the Eucharist
    are a valuable means to grace
    when entered into with faith.
We wish to encourage further dialogue and understanding
    about the importance and meaning
    of both baptism and Eucharist.

23 Liturgy and prayer, which in many communities
    express our common roots,
    are another aspect of Christian life
        which could be a basis for more unity.
Such worship is often the starting point
    for great works of charity
        and a lively faith life.
Those who worship and pray together
    often find that the next step
        is to serve others together.
A life of charity that is based on the Gospel
    can give witness to the common call
        of all Christians.
Hence, using the Gospel as a starting point
    for applying faith to everyday life
    is another basis for forming ties of unity.

24 While this council strongly encourages
    ecumenical activity,

it once again cautions against false ecumenism.
In all matters, Catholics must be clear about their own faith
   so as not to give the impression of a communion
      that does not really exist.
Closing our eyes and pretending
   does not make our dream of unity
   a reality.
Such activities actually hinder rather than help
   the movement to reestablish Christian unity.

In the end, we want to acknowledge
   that the work of ecumenism
   is really the work of the Holy Spirit.
We are called to be instruments of that work,
   but it is beyond human power to achieve it.
We must recognize that, as in all of Christian life,
   we ultimately depend on the goodness of God.
We believe that Christ fervently desires unity
   and that in God's own time,
      such unity will come to exist
      through the power of the Holy Spirit.

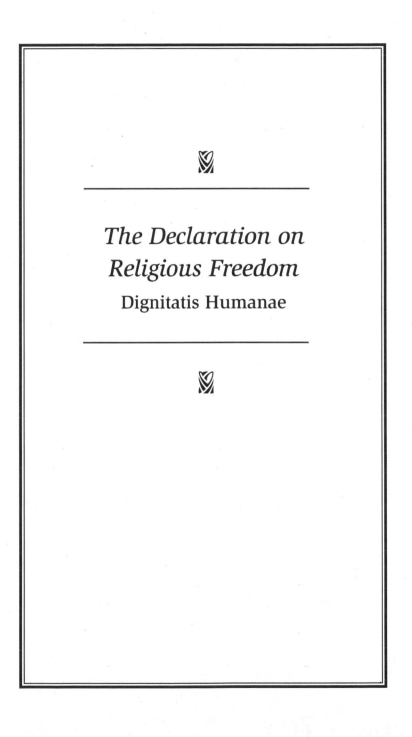

The Declaration on Religious Freedom

Dignitatis Humanae

Chapter Three

※

PART ONE: BACKGROUND

The first version of this document was submitted to the council for consideration on November 19, 1963. After that, the council fathers considered no less than five fully revised versions, each prepared by the commission responsible for this work. Those working on revisions took into account the more than six hundred comments and 2,000 amendments proposed by the council fathers in the course of three public debates, countless discussions, and debates around the city of Rome and the world.

As John Courtney Murray said, this was the most extensive discussion on religious freedom ever held in the history of the Church. The free and vigorous debate led sometimes to greater confusion and other times to greater clarity. Why was the *Declaration on Religious Freedom* the most controversial document at the council? Partly because it raised the issue of the development of doctrine, an issue that was beneath the surface in most council debates.

This document brought to an end a long-standing contradiction in Catholic teaching: that the Catholic Church has freedom to preach the Gospel, but no other Church has the freedom to preach its doctrines, especially when the other Church is non-Christian.

Still it must be noted that, although the idea of religious liberty is not being proclaimed here for the first time, the

Church is rather late in doing so. At least a hundred nations of the world guarantee religious freedom constitutionally and some have done so for many centuries.

Even the United Nations affirmed this right in its *Universal Declaration of Human Rights* adopted in 1948. Many other charters and documents around the world also do this. The World Council of Churches itself proclaimed this right in its *Amsterdam Declaration* in 1948 and again in its *New Delhi Statement* in 1961.

This declaration of the Catholic Church, then, takes its place among others in the world and is one of the most important doctrinal statements of the council, as Pope Paul VI himself pointed out in his remarks as it was being promulgated.

Prior to Vatican II, the Church did not provide religious freedom to other religions in nations that were firmly Catholic, yet it demanded freedom for itself in nations that were not mainly Catholic. The first schema on the Church, prepared before the council began, proposed this contradictory approach as the status quo. However, the council fathers rejected the document in the first days of its consideration.

Hence, work on the *Declaration on Religious Freedom* began only over the serious objections of curial insiders and with explicit permission of Pope John XXIII and the tireless efforts of the courageous Cardinal Bea and Monsignor Jan Willebrands in the Secretariat for Promoting Christian Unity.

In the end, the vote to approve this document for promulgation came on December 7, 1965, the day before the Second Vatican Council adjourned, and the count fell 2,308 in favor and 70 opposed.

In a sense, nothing "new" is declared here, yet because freedom in matters religious is declared publicly and in a spirit of ecumenism, it brings a great deal that is new to the life of the Church. More debate will surely follow.

PART TWO: PARAPHRASE TEXT

*F*rom the Vatican II document
promulgated on December 7, 1965

On the Right of the Person and of Communities to Social and Civil Freedom in Matters Religious

[1] There is an increasing sense
  among modern people
  of the basic dignity of the human person.
Also increasing is the demand
  that people have the right to act
  on their own judgment,
  using and savoring their innate freedom
    without coercion.
Likewise, there is an increasing demand
  that governments limit their powers
  and not encroach on this freedom,
    for persons or groups.
This drive for greater freedom
  is especially evident
  in the free exercise of religion.
We here in this council
  now intend to declare these human desires
  and to probe our tradition on this matter.

First and foremost, we believe that God
    is the source of human understanding
    which leads to service and salvation.
  Believing in this and having faith in God this way
    is what defines the term *religion*.
We believe that this religion subsists
    in the catholic and apostolic Church,
    which is to say that we hold it to be true
    that the Church is where we meet and worship God
        and go forth to spread the word
            about that truth.

Christ himself commanded his followers
    in Matthew's Gospel
    to go and make disciples of all nations,
    to baptize all people,
        and to teach all that Jesus taught.
We believe that all men and women are therefore
    required to seek the truth
    and, once found, to adhere to it steadfastly.
This obligation to seek the truth
    is found in each person's conscience,
    where, under its own power,
        the truth makes itself known
        with both force
            and gentle peace.
Religious liberty, as we speak of it here,
    refers to that condition of existence
    in which men and women experience this inner truth
        without coercion in civil society
        and with absolute freedom.
In this declaration, we intend to elaborate and develop
    the doctrine about this matter
    as given by previous popes.

Part One: General Principle of Religious Freedom

2 The Second Vatican Council hereby declares
 that human beings have a right
 to religious liberty.
This means that no one is to be forced
 by other individuals,
  by social groups,
  or by any other human power
   regarding religious matters.
No one should ever be forced to act
 in a way that is contrary
 to his or her beliefs.
Nor should anyone ever be kept from acting
 according to those beliefs,
  whether in private or in public,
   alone or in a social group,
   within appropriate limits.
This right is rooted in the nature
 of what it means to be human;
 it is founded in human dignity,
  which is made known to us
  both through the revealed Word
  and by reason.
This right should be assured constitutionally,
 that is, it should be written into civil law
  as a basic human right everywhere on earth.

All women and men are obliged to seek the truth
 by their very natures as humans.
We humans are, after all,
 given reason and free will;
 we are given a sense of personal duty.
We are thus duty-bound to seek the truth

and to order our lives
according to its demands.
This is the reason why religious liberty
is so important.
For how can someone do this
if he or she is coerced
either from outside himself or herself
or from within?
Therefore, we can say with confidence that
free, intelligent, and reasonable human persons
must be allowed their freedom
whether they exercise it or not,
but they must also be responsible.

3 Humans are created by God
and participate in the rest of God's created world,
which has its own laws:
eternal,
objective,
and universal.
All of life and the world is governed by God
according to these laws,
and humans come more and more to see this.
Under God's guiding hand, in other words,
human beings discover the truth.
Because of this,
every person has the duty to seek truth
in order that he or she might properly form
his or her conscience
and follow the plan of God for human life.
This pursuit of the truth
is to be done freely and in dialogue with others
as well as through formal instruction.
By reflecting on one's conscience,

people arrive at an understanding of truth,
and once perceived,
    one is obliged to follow that truth
    which always leads to God.
We conclude from this belief
    that no one should be forced
        to act against his or her conscience
        nor restrained from following it.
Religion, furthermore, is the turning of the heart
    toward God,
    which is always a voluntary act
    on the part of human beings.
And humans often feel compelled to share this
    in religious acts of worship and action
    and are injured when that is not permitted.
Governments should ensure that religion is freely practiced
    but should avoid either directing
        or preventing
        religion from being followed.

4 The individual right to be free from coercion
    in matters religious
    also extends to communities
    where religious bodies organize themselves.
Such religious bodies have the right
    to control their activity
    (provided the public order is maintained)
    and to worship, teach, and promote their beliefs.
They likewise have the right to choose and train
    their own ministers,
    communicate with their worldwide members,
    and hold and use funds for their purposes.
They may also witness to their faith
    both in writing and in broadcast media.

In this, religious people should avoid
　　the appearance of coercion themselves,
　　nor should they use methods of persuasion
　　　　that are beneath human dignity
　　　　especially among the uneducated and poor.
They are also free to hold meetings,
　　to establish various organizations,
　　and to follow their religious impulse.
And, finally, religious people have the right
　　to submit to the public solutions,
　　to human and social problems,
　　which spring from their beliefs.

5 The family,
　　a small society of its own,
　　also has a right to live according
　　　　to its own religious inclinations,
　　　　guided by the parents,
　　　　who have the right to train their children.
Governments should insure this
　　and should not force children
　　to attend religious instruction
　　　　that their parents do not want.
But governments also should not prevent
　　the teaching of religion
　　in appropriate ways.

6 It is in the interest of everyone to protect these rights
　　and it is the duty of the whole citizenry
　　　　to defend them.
Principally this duty belongs to government,
　　which enacts just laws
　　and enforces them well.
Even if one particular religious group dominates

in a nation or region,
all other groups should likewise be assured
   their freedoms
   and no discrimination should fall upon those
   who practice a nonmajority religion.
Force should never enter into government's practices
   in this regard,
   whether to promote or repress any religion.

7 Religion is not a purely private action.
It is practiced within human society
   and requires that everyone respect
   each other's religious choices.
The moral law of personal and social responsibility
   comes into play in this regard
   and binds people to justice and civility
      in dealing with one another.
Some people will abuse this right to religious freedom
   and masquerade as religionists
   while really being something quite different.
When that happens, governments must, of course,
   regulate the abuse of this right,
   but its regulation must be fair and impartial.
By providing such regulatory safeguards,
   governments protect those
   who practice religion honestly.
Furthermore, all true religion benefits
   by providing for peaceful settlement
   when there is conflict among competing rights
   and by providing for a society
      in which people can live with civil order,
         true justice,
         and public morality.

8 There are so many pressures on modern people
   that it is sometimes difficult
   to know one's conscience
      and act with freedom.
On the other hand,
   some people today use the name of freedom
   in order to do whatever they please,
      without regard to authority.
We here at Vatican II urge everyone, therefore,
   especially those in education,
   to form women and men who love true freedom:
      people coming to their own decisions,
      using their own judgment,
      following the light of truth,
      being responsible seekers of goodness,
      and cooperating with others toward that end.
True freedom, then, results in people
   who act with greater responsibility
   in fulfilling their obligations to the community.

Part Two: Religious Freedom in the Light of Revelation

9 Our declaration of the right to religious liberty
   is founded in the dignity of the human person,
   which has, through the centuries,
      become more and more evident
      to human reason.
It is also founded in divine revelation,
   giving Christians a special duty to honor it.
Revelation does not explicitly claim this right,
   but it does establish human dignity
   as its main theme
      and shows that Christ himself
      demonstrated this for us.

10 Catholicism has always taught as a main doctrine
     that human faith and response to God
          must first and foremost be free.
Therefore, as we have already said over and over,
     no one is to be forced to embrace Christianity
     against his or her will.
If the heart is not moved in freedom,
     what does faith contain but empty words?
How can one consent to belief
     if the consent is forced
     and the faith is not free?
By its very nature, the call to faith is a call to freedom,
     and allowing people their freedom
     will increase, not decrease,
          the number who embrace Christ.
11 For even though God calls everyone
     to return to God in spirit and truth,
     God also allows people freedom,
          to choose to do that or not.
In Christ, we have a high example of this
     because he acted with patience toward all,
     especially his disciples.
He aroused belief through his personal presence,
     and through his teachings,
          healings,
          and loving ways,
               but not through force.
Indeed, he rejected the unbelief of those
     whose hearts were hardened to him,
     but he left their judgment to God
     and gave orders that the wheat and the weeds
          should both be allowed to grow to harvest,
          where they would be separated appropriately.
He rejected the title of political ruler,

preferring the way of service,
and, while acknowledging the place of government,
    nonetheless ordered that what is of God
    should be given back to God.
And in the end, he chose to persuade us to believe
    by offering his life rather than forcing his way.
        Hence, he bore witness to the truth
        but did not impose it on anyone.
His disciples followed Christ in this
    and preferred the power of their witness
    to methods of ministry that force others,
        or manipulate them,
        into belief.
They proclaimed the Word of Faith,
    while at the same time they realized that each person
    must make his or her own accounting with God
    and is, therefore, bound to follow conscience.

The apostles preached the Word of God
    with full confidence that it contains within it
    ample divine power to attract believers
        and to destroy all that is ungodly.
They at once respected governmental authority
    and rejected any governmental powers
    that moved against the Word,
    saying explicitly in chapter five of Acts:
        "We must obey God rather than people." (5:29)
Countless martyrs and other witnesses to the faith
    have followed this same course
    down through the centuries.

12 At certain times in the history of the Church,
    we ourselves have not allowed for this freedom
    when preaching the Word and spreading the faith.

At certain times, our ways of behaving
    were in downright opposition to the Gospels.
Nevertheless, we have never ceased teaching
    that coercion has no place in faith
    and we ourselves have grown in understanding
        and applying this principle.

13 The Church itself should be given the same freedom
    that we are discussing here—
    freedom to do its work as it sees fit.
To prevent the Church from having this freedom
    is to act against the will of God
    expressed in Christ,
        who purchased this freedom
        with his blood.
We, therefore, claim this freedom as our own
    so that we can preach the Gospel everywhere,
    so that we can love and serve God everywhere,
    and so that we can live in society with each other
        as the Body of Christ, everywhere.

14 What is it we ask of our own members
    in the area of religious liberty?
We ask that they, first of all,
    pray steadfastly as the First Letter to Timothy says,
    "because this is good and agreeable
        in the sight of God." (2:1–4)
We ask, furthermore, that as they form their consciences,
    Christians carefully consider the doctrines
        of the Church,
        which teaches as Christ did
        and leads all to truth.
And even more, we ask that all Christians
    give witness to this truth,

spreading the Light of Christ with urgency.
In performing these tasks of witnessing,
    the disciple of Christ is bound
    to a balanced approach,
        one that never uses means which contradict
        or are incompatible with the Gospel itself.

The disciple is to act lovingly,
    with prudence and patience,
    taking into account the command to preach
        while balancing that with the innate freedom
        in those to whom the preaching is offered.

15 In sum, we observe that religious freedom
    is already being recognized by most governments
    and is a desire of all modern people.
But forms of government still exist that do not allow it,
    and we meet this fact with sorrow.
We denounce this effort to prevent people
    from having liberty in religious matters,
    and we plead for greater freedom everywhere.
As nations work more and more together,
    we urge that freedom be provided everywhere
    and that respect be given to this aspect
        of human nature.
May God provide that as men and women grow in freedom,
    they will likewise grow in faith.

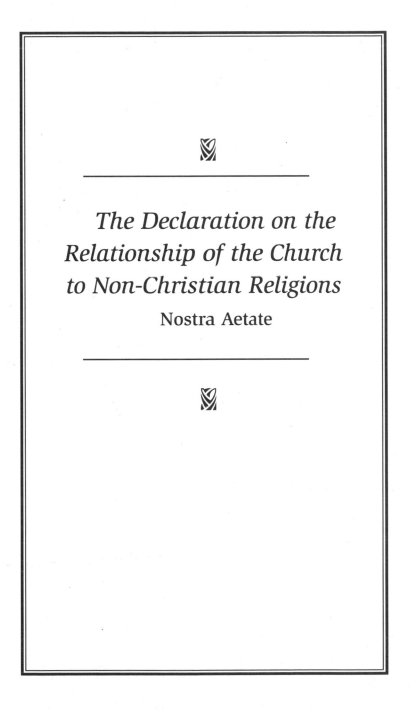

The Declaration on the Relationship of the Church to Non-Christian Religions

Nostra Aetate

Chapter Four

⁂

PART ONE: BACKGROUND

*P*erhaps no Vatican II document had a more complex course to promulgation than this one. Pope John XXIII strongly desired that the council make a statement on the Jews. Sensitive to history and deeply aware of anti-Semitism, Pope John asked Augustin Cardinal Bea to take charge of this task. Nearly the same age as Pope John, Cardinal Bea was a brilliant scholar and a skilled diplomat whom Pope John trusted.

The present document began as chapter four in the original schema on ecumenism, which was submitted to the council for the first time on November 18, 1963. Although this occurred after the death of Pope John, Cardinal Bea made clear to the council fathers that the deceased pope wished to have such a statement. In fact, Pope John had seen and approved the major lines of thought in the *Declaration on the Relationship of the Church to Non-Christian Religions* before his death.

A movement arose among the council fathers to separate the questions on non-Christians from those on Christian ecumenism. Likewise, they moved material on religious liberty, contained in chapter five of the original schema on ecumenism, to a separate document.

In the period between the second and third sessions (the spring and summer of 1964), Cardinal Bea and his commission prepared the new document on the Jews and other non-Christians. The text they prepared explicitly said that the Jews were not guilty of "deicide," which means "the killing of God." For centuries, the Jews had been hated, marginalized, and murdered in mass numbers because Christians accused them of deicide, but the first draft of the *Declaration on the Relationship of the Church to Non-Christian Religions* brought that charge to its formal end.

Throughout the world, newspapers published this material before the council fathers had even seen much of it. However, when the third session of Vatican II convened, the document submitted to the council fathers did not contain the denial of "deicide." It had disappeared! Furthermore, the sections of the documents dealing with non-Christians other than Jews had been broadened, especially the part dealing with the Moslems.

A long list of cardinals and bishops from all parts of the world called loudly for the explicit term *deicide* to be returned to the document. (Apparently, "editors" working within Vatican circles between the commission's final meeting and the opening of the third session itself had removed the word.) In the end, the term was not returned to the document.

The present document was approved by a vote of 2,221 to 88 and promulgated on October 28, 1965.

PART TWO: PARAPHRASE TEXT

*F*rom the Vatican II document
promulgated on October 28, 1965

1 In our day and age,
    people everywhere are growing closer together,
    and their ties are becoming more profound,
        even when they are socially diverse.
Because of this reality, the Church is giving more attention
        to its relationship with non-Christian religions
        and, toward that end, gives primary consideration
            in this document
            to what unites all people
            and to what people have in common.
This furthers the Church's task of fostering unity and love
        among people
        and even among various nations.
For we believe and teach
        that all men and women form one human family,
        have a common origin in God,
        and share a common destiny in divine providence.
People naturally look to various religions
        to answer profound human questions:
            What does it mean to be human?
            What is goodness? What is sin?
            What makes us sad?
            What is the path to happiness?
            What does death mean?
            What is beyond the grave?
            What, in short, is the mystery of life?

2 People have long sensed
        the presence of the divine,
        however that is understood or defined.
It seems to hover near us,
        mysteriously present in the events of life.
We have variously known this as a supreme being—

a divinity or heavenly sort of parent—
and this has given people a religious sense.
In Hinduism, for example,
 people contemplate this divine mystery
 and speak of it through myths
  and penetrating inquiry,
  seeking relief of human struggle
   through ascetical practice,
   meditation,
   or movement toward God.
In various forms of Buddhism, too,
 people understand that the current situation
  is not sufficient
  and that there is a path for life
  on which people can reach greater freedom
  or enlightenment.
In many other religions around the world as well,
 people strive to relieve their restless hearts
 through religious practices and lifestyles
  that consist of teachings,
   rules of life,
   and sacred rites.
The Catholic Church does not reject anything
 that is true and holy in any of these religions
 and, in fact, looks upon them
  with sincere respect.
Even though they differ from us,
 their ways of life and doctrines
 often reflect the truth that we all seek.
The Church, of course, continues to proclaim Christ
 as "the way, the truth, and the life,"
 but we also exhort all our members
  to be prudent and loving
  and open to dialogue with others.

We urge Christians to defend and promote
 the spiritual and moral benefits
 found among other world religions,
 including the values found in their cultures.

3 We also appreciate the Moslems,
 who adore one God who, they believe,
 acts with mercy and power,
 who is our creator and sustainer.
They seek to obey God
 in the spirit of Abraham and Sarah,
 even when the divine decrees seem inscrutable.
Even though they do not believe in the divinity of Jesus,
 nonetheless they revere him as a prophet,
 and they honor Mary, his mother.
They wait with us for the judgment day,
 when God will give all their due,
 and therefore, they value a moral life
 and practice prayer, fasting, and almsgiving.
Even though we have had many hostilities
 between Christians and Moslems,
 we now urge all to forget the past
 and work for mutual understanding and peace.

4 This council also recalls the spiritual bonds
 that unite Christians and Jews:
 our common heritage in Sarah and Abraham.
We are the Church of Christ,
 but we acknowledge that the roots of our faith
 are in the spiritual ancestors,
  Moses,
  and the prophets
   whom we hold in common.
The very story of Christianity—

that God is leading us to freedom—
was foreshadowed by the journey of the Jews
    from bondage to freedom
    through the desert.
We cannot forget, therefore,
    that we received divine revelation
    through the Jews.
They are, after all, the ones chosen by God,
    the ones to whom God offered mercy
    and the ancient covenant.
As Christians, we are rooted in Judaism,
    and we even believe that in Christ,
    Jew and Gentile were reconciled
        once and for all.
Mary herself was a Jew, of course,
    as were all the apostles,
    not to mention Christ himself—
        a faithful Jew.
The Church's very foundation
    was laid among the Jews,
        as Paul said in the ninth chapter
        of his Letter to the Romans.
The Jews, he said,
    have been adopted as daughters and sons;
    they have been given a covenant,
        have been given a divine law,
        have been taught to worship God,
        and, indeed, have been given Christ.

And, while certain ones among first-century Jews
    did not accept the Gospel
    and some outrightly opposed its spread,
    nevertheless the Jews remain dear to God,
        who never takes back a gift

and who has given the Jews many!
God likewise never takes back a decision,
    and God has decided to choose the Jews
        as history clearly reveals.

We now wait for that day on which all people
    will come together to worship,
        but that day is known only to God.
Because of this huge and rich shared heritage,
    we in this council wish to foster and recommend
    mutual understanding and respect,
        biblical and theological study,
        and intimate dialogue between us.
For even though certain Jews did favor
    and press for the death of Jesus,
        that death cannot rightly be blamed on all Jews
        either living then
        or, certainly, living now.
Although we believe that the Church
    is now the new People of God,
    the Jews are not hated and rejected by God.
        They are not cursed by God!
No one should teach this
    and claim it is based in Scripture,
    for that is simply and completely wrong.
We reject completely any persecution
    against the Jews,
    and we deplore the hatred,
        persecution
        and anti-Semitism of the past.
Beyond that, we teach that Christ chose his death
    with freedom and love for us
    in order to free us from slavery
        and lead us to salvation.

The cross is, therefore, a sign of love
and a fountain of grace.

5 It is really not possible to call upon God,
the creator and sustainer of all,
if we treat anyone less than lovingly.
The Scriptures themselves say as much
when they remind us that whoever does not love
does not know God,
because God is love.
Hence, one's relationship to God
is intimately linked to one's relationship
to those around him or her.
There is absolutely no ground, then,
to offer anyone less than full dignity and respect.
Therefore, we outrightly reject and abhor
any discrimination against anyone
based on race,
color,
condition of life,
or religion.

We beg all Christians
to be at peace
and to maintain good relations
with all peoples.

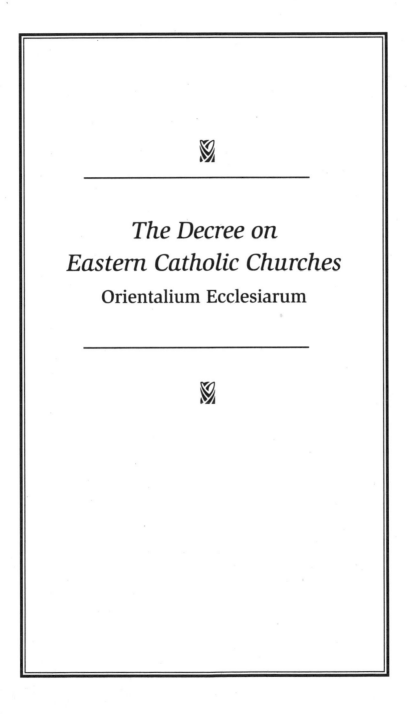

The Decree on
Eastern Catholic Churches
Orientalium Ecclesiarum

Chapter Five

⬚

PART ONE: BACKGROUND

*T*here are two kinds of Eastern Churches: those that are Catholic and those that are not. The Eastern Catholic Churches have six main branches and twenty-one rites. They differ from the Latin Rite because of ancient traditions.

The non-Catholic Eastern Churches are known as either Greek or Russian Eastern Orthodox Rites.

The original schema dealing with the Eastern Churches dealt mainly with the Catholic Rites and was circulated at the council on November 30, 1962. It was not approved at that time, however. Why? Because some council fathers wanted to combine the schema with others that dealt with ecumenical questions, specifically those concerning Protestants and Anglicans. The idea of combining the schemata was eventually deemed inadequate for the weight of this matter, however.

Following the first session, therefore, those working on this document rewrote it with a focus once again on Eastern Catholic Churches. They resubmitted the revised document for debate on October 15, 1964. But once again, the council fathers, especially the Eastern prelates themselves, found the schema unacceptable. In general, they felt that it did not deal sufficiently with the place of the patriarchs in the Eastern Catholic Churches and that it sounded more Roman than ecumenical.

Nearly 2,000 suggested changes were submitted at that time, and the council approved the final document, revised for the third time, by a vote of 2,110 to 39. The pope promulgated it on November 21, 1964.

In the end, this document deals with both those Eastern Churches that are Catholic and those that are not. It offers a generous and more lenient sharing of pastoral ministries with those who are not Catholic and holds out an open posture that it hopes will lead to reunion.

Also, the decree more generously allows for diversity within the Catholic Church when addressing the Eastern Churches, some of whom have practices, such as marriage of the clergy, that vary greatly from those in the Roman Church of the West.

In doing this, the bishops may have established a model for ecumenism-based-on-diversity, rather than ecumenism that expects absolute conformity in every detail of worship and church life.

This document should be read in tandem with the decree on ecumenism.

PART TWO: PARAPHRASE TEXT

*F*rom the Vatican II document
promulgated on November 21, 1964

Concerning the Eastern Churches That Are Catholic

1 The Catholic Church

holds dear the Eastern Churches
that have remained in union with the pope,
    including their rites of worship,
    their traditions of governance,
    and their Christian way of life.
They are ancient Churches,
    and they shine with their traditions,
    which have come down from the apostles
    through the early Fathers and Mothers
        of the Church.
Indeed, they are part of the undivided Church,
    based on the revealed truths of our faith.
We intend here to give some principles
    to assist in their life
    so they might grow and prosper
    and accomplish their mission.
We leave certain other matters
    to Eastern synods and the pope.

2 The Church is composed of its faithful
    (laypeople, religious, and clergy),
    who are bound together by the Spirit,
        share the same sacraments,
        live under the same governance,
        and, united under the hierarchy,
            form several distinct Churches.

Having the variety within the Church,
    which results from the presence
    of these various Churches,
        deepens our own unity
        because it shows that diversity
            is indeed welcome here.
We encourage each church group

(whether the Eastern or the Western Rites)
to retain its own customs and style
while correcting itself to meet the needs of today.

3 All of these Churches,
including both those in the East
and those in the West,
have equal dignity
and are held in equal esteem by the pope.
They, in fact, have the same mission:
to preach the Gospel!

4 Because of this,
in places where they share the same geographic area,
they should cooperate at every level
for the good of all.
All seminarians should be trained to understand well
the various rites of the Church.
And those who enter the Church
should remain in their own particular rite
and follow it as closely as possible.

5 The whole universal Church is deeply indebted
to the Eastern traditions,
and we now declare that each Church
should rule itself
for the good of its people.

6 Therefore, all those in the Eastern Churches
should be assured that they can preserve
their liturgical rites and ways of life.
In fact, where parts of that have been lost,
they should be restored.
And those who have contact with the Eastern Churches

should understand and respect them as well.

7 There has always been one named patriarch
    who governs all bishops of each Church
    without undermining the primacy of the pope.
8 All patriarchs in the East are of equal dignity,
    although there is a clear order of precedence.
9 The patriarchs with their synods
    are the first authority in their dioceses,
    known in the East as "eparchies."
Their rites and privileges should be restored
    and adapted to these times.
10 The same is true for archbishops.
11 Where needed, new patriarchates should be erected
    by a council or the pope.

12 We applaud the tradition of having sacraments
    which exists in the Eastern Churches
    and call for them to be restored.
13 In the East, priests may confer confirmation
    provided they use oil blessed
        by a bishop or patriarch.
14 All priests of the East may confer valid baptism
    on anyone, including those in the West,
    and priests of the West may likewise
        confer valid baptism on those in the East.
In both cases, the sacrament is "licit"
    only if the priest follows the law carefully.
15 All the faithful are bound to attend Mass
    on Sundays and major feasts,
    according to the rules of their particular Church,
    but they may meet this obligation
        on Saturday evening
        or anytime on Sunday itself.

16 Any priest may celebrate reconciliation
   with any Catholic of any Church.

17 We urge the East to restore
   the office of the permanent deacon.
18 Marriages between Eastern Catholics
   and Eastern non-Catholics are valid
      if a priest is present,
      although certain legal factors pertain.

19 The setting or changing of feast days
   observed in all the Eastern Churches
   is done by a council or the pope.
20 We leave it to local patriarchs to set the date
   for Easter.
21 People living away from the main body of their Church
   may observe Advent-Christmastide
   and Lent-Eastertide according to local dating,
      and when members of a single family
      belong to more than one Church,
      they may choose any one set of rules.
22 Eastern Catholics should celebrate the Divine Praises
   according to their local tradition.
23 Local patriarchs may determine the proper language
   and also approve translations of texts.

Concerning the Eastern Churches That Are Not Catholic

24 Eastern Catholic Churches have a key role to play
   in establishing Christian unity through
      prayer,
      the example of their lives,
      fidelity to ancient traditions,
      greater mutual knowledge of one another,

collaboration,
and a kind regard for objects and attitudes.

25 If someone from one of the separated Eastern Churches
chooses to become Catholic,
he or she will be asked
only for a simple profession of faith.

The clergy of those Churches are validly ordained
and may exercise their ministry according
to standard regulations,
and all their baptisms are likewise valid.

26 Divine law prohibits sharing sacraments
in such a way that church unity is harmed,
but we take pastoral needs into account today
and offer this new principle:

27 Eastern Christians separated from the Catholic Church
may request and be given the sacraments
of penance,
Eucharist,
and the anointing of the sick.

Likewise, Catholics may request such
from separated Eastern ministers when necessary
and when access to a Catholic priest
is not available.

28 Catholics may also join with separated Eastern Christians
in sacred functions, things, and places.

29 Local bishops may issue rules to govern
this more lenient policy.

Conclusion

30 We await the day when we will be in full unity
with our separated sisters and brothers

in the Eastern non-Catholic Churches.
We urge all in both Churches to pray for this day
as Paul asks in the Letter to the Romans
that we love one another with fond affection
like sisters and brothers,
outdoing one another in showing honor.

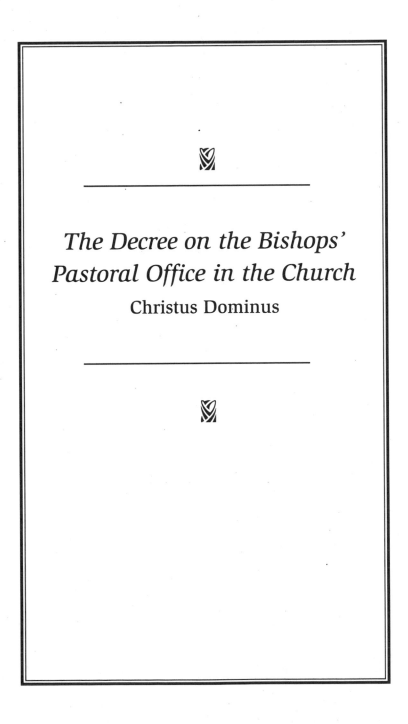

The Decree on the Bishops' Pastoral Office in the Church

Christus Dominus

Chapter Six

※

PART ONE: BACKGROUND

No office in the Church has been more troublesome nor any more helpful in the spread of the Gospel than the office of the bishop. Moreover, none has been so poorly understood as this one.

At the time of the Council of Trent in the sixteenth century, the office of bishop had fallen into terrible disrepair. We need not recount the many abuses prevalent then, nor the lack of pastoral concern that many bishops demonstrated in the discharge of their duties. The implementation of the decrees of the Council of Trent, however, recharged the episcopacy and it was the bishops who carried the rubrics of Trent to the far corners of the earth, becoming fervent almost overnight in the application of the discipline and order that Trent demanded.

In the late nineteenth century, the First Vatican Council ended abruptly in the midst of its business, having yielded to conservative forces which insisted on a clear definition of papal power and supremacy. That same council may have also reviewed the office of bishop had not advancing armies sent the participants scampering home.

Following Vatican I, the papacy became more and more powerful, and the offices of the Roman Curia benefited. Those officials were charged, after all, with carrying out the triumphant power of Rome all over the world, and they did so with relish.

Especially during an unhappy period at the turn of the century, these Roman officials had priests turning in their own brother priests for minor variances from the law. Theologians who dared speak up were silenced, judged, and sometimes exiled. Appointments were made among trusted insiders and were denied to bishops who seemed too liberal.

As the preparations for Vatican II got under way, everyone who understood the need for the reform of the office of bishop in the Church assumed this would be a major outcome of the council. But the Curia in Rome did everything it could, right up to the last minute, to thwart any such reform. They sincerely believed that they, and only they, were competent to govern the Church.

The *Decree on the Bishops' Pastoral Office in the Church* began as one called "On the Care of Souls" and retained much of the language of that schema. Chapter three of the *Dogmatic Constitution on the Church* also treats the topic of the bishops' pastoral office, but this latter document is more specific as it gives a "job description" for bishops. The decree relies on the theology developed in the constitution on the Church.

And even though the decree necessarily speaks of the "power" of bishops, its tone suggests almost the opposite: that bishops stand among their people as servants. This document calls for self-denial and self-sacrifice on behalf of the faithful and repeats over and over again that the guiding principle in the organization of the Church is the care of souls, an echo of the abandoned document from which the *Decree on the Bishops' Pastoral Office in the Church* flowed.

Continuing the work done in chapter three of the constitution on the Church, the main advance of the *Decree on the Bishops' Pastoral Office in the Church* is the definition of "collegiality." That is, the council calls on the bishops and the pope to advance the Gospel by working together as a community just as the apostles did. This idea, so deeply rooted in Scripture, had been lost for fifteen centuries!

Indeed! From the time when Constantine created a centralized church government, the relationship of bishops to the pope has been fuzzy. This document, however, stands as a milepost in church history. It passed by a final vote of 2,319 for and 2 against. It was promulgated on October 28, 1965.

PART TWO: PARAPHRASE TEXT

*F*rom theVatican II document
promulgated on October 28, 1965

Introduction

1 The mission of Jesus Christ
    was to show us the way to life
    and assist us in being holy.
He sent the apostles to continue that work,
    and he offered them the Holy Spirit
    as a help and guide
        so that the Church would be fortified.
2 In Christ's Church,
    the bishop of Rome, the pope,
    is the successor of Peter,
        whom Christ had made leader.
The pope is, therefore, pastor of all,
    with supreme,

full,
immediate,
and universal authority
over the care of souls.
The pope's job is to provide for the common good
of the universal Church
as well as the good of individual Churches.
Bishops have also been appointed
by the Holy Spirit
and are successors of the apostles
as the pastors of souls.
They work with the pope
and under his authority
as true and authentic teachers of the faith.

3 All the bishops are united in a "college," or body,
although they exercise their authority individually
in the particular local Church entrusted to them.

Aware of the changing times
and the needs of our modern world,
we issue this decree to more accurately describe
the pastoral office of the bishop.

Chapter One
THE RELATIONSHIP OF BISHOPS
TO THE UNIVERSAL CHURCH

4 When a bishop is chosen and consecrated,
he becomes part of the episcopal body.
As we said in the *Dogmatic Constitution on the Church*,
there has been no break

in the succession of bishops
from the apostles until now.
Together with the pope,
and never without him,
the body of bishops has full power
over the universal Church.
This power is used at councils such as this one
in a very solemn manner.
And this power can also be used outside of a council
when the pope calls it into action
or ratifies a united action of bishops
to make it truly collegiate.

5 On another level, bishops will be chosen
to serve in a special, smaller council,
to be known as the "Synod of Bishops"
which will assist the pope in his duties
and act in the name of all bishops.

6 Bishops are responsible for the entire Church
in addition to their own dioceses.
7 Therefore, they should
promote evangelization worldwide,
send suitable ministers to the missions,
offer financial assistance to poor dioceses
and to the afflicted in times of disasters,
and take an active interest in bishops
who are oppressed and imprisoned.

8 Bishops have all the power they need
to govern their dioceses,
but this power never infringes on that of the pope.
Unless specifically reserved to the pope,
bishops may give dispensations to the faithful
provided they follow the law in doing so

and when they think it is pastorally beneficial.
9 The pope makes use of various offices
    at the Vatican called "the Curia"
    to help him govern the Church,
        and the bishops of this council
        urge a reorganization of the Curia.
We hope it can be better adapted to these times
    as well as to the needs of the world.
We also think it would be helpful
    to determine more precisely
    the role of papal legates in various nations.
10 We also think it would be wise
    to choose people to serve in the Curia
    from a wider geographic area
        so the offices will reflect
        a truly universal character.
It would also be a benefit, we think,
    to employ diocesan bishops more
    because their advice would be closer
        to the actual needs of the local scene.
And finally, we recommend that the Curia
    listen more closely to laypeople
    who have a share in church affairs as well.

Chapter Two
BISHOPS AND THEIR PARTICULAR CHURCHES OR DIOCESES

1. Diocesan Bishops

11 A diocese is a portion of the faithful
    which is entrusted to a bishop, who is its shepherd,

along with his priests and deacons.
The Church is truly present in each diocese
    through the Gospel and the Eucharist.
The bishops are under the authority of the pope,
    which we have already stated,
        but they should allow for the rights
            of patriarchs and other authorities.
Bishops have the care of the faithful as their charge,
    including those who have left the Church
    or those who have not yet heard the Gospel.

12 Here are the duties of the bishop as we see them:
First and foremost,
    bishops announce the Gospel to all,
    teach the mysteries we believe,
    and help people attain heavenly bliss.
They are to show that the things of this earth
    can contribute to the plan of God
    and the growth of the Body of Christ.
They are to demonstrate the Church's serious regard
    for the human person's freedom and life,
    for the family and the place of children there,
    for civil society and its legal and professional life,
    for labor and leisure,
        arts,
        technology,
        poverty and affluence,
        war and peace,
        justice and the common good of all.
13 They are to adapt the presentation of our doctrine
    to the needs of today,
    so it addresses people in their most real lives.
They are to seek out those who have needs,
    especially the poor,

and foster dialogue with all people.
Toward this end, their speech should be clear,
    and their approach a thoroughly modern one,
    making use of every avenue available today
        to preach the Gospel to all.

14 They are to insure that children receive formation
    based on Scripture,
        the Liturgy,
        the Church's teachings,
        and the life of the Church.
Toward this end, they are to ensure that catechists
    are properly trained
    and catechumens given more suitable preparation.
15 They are to be constantly mindful
    that they have the fullness of holy orders
    and that, therefore, their chief duty
        is to make present the Eucharist
        along with the other sacraments,
            working with the priests and deacons
            of their dioceses.
Toward this end, they are to foster the holiness
    of the clergy, religious, and laity in their midst
    and give an example themselves
        of charity,
        humility,
        and simplicity of life.
16 In carrying out the duties of his office,
    a bishop stands among his people
    as one who serves.
He is to be a shepherd who knows his sheep
    and loves them,
    gathering all who minister into one flock.
Toward this end, bishops must live

as "men of these times."
Bishops are to regard priests as sons and friends,
    as well as coworkers.
Toward this end, the bishop should provide the means
    in the local diocese
        through which the priests can grow in faith,
            live holy lives,
            and fulfill their ministry faithfully.
He should hold special conferences for priests
    from time to time
        in which they can gain theological insight,
            fraternal support,
            and new methods of pastoral work.
And the bishop is to approach troubled priests
    with mercy.
The bishop must be aware of the life of the faithful
    who are under his care.
Toward this end, he is to consult social research
    and make every suitable effort
        to understand the needs of various groups
        and be aware of their baptismal right and duty
            to work in the apostolate.
Finally, the bishop should offer love
    to our separated sisters and brothers
        and urge all members of the Church
            to do likewise.
He should also care about the nonbaptized
    with the same generous love.

17 The bishop is to foster and encourage the apostolate
    in all its many possible forms
    and provide a harmonizing role within the diocese.
Toward this end, the faithful should be urged
    to assume their various duties,

each according to his or her gifts.
The way in which ministry is carried out
    should be adapted to the modern times,
    and the use of social surveys to assist that
        is cordially recommended.
18 The bishop is to pay special attention to those
    who cannot avail themselves
    of usual pastoral services,
        especially immigrants,
            migrants,
            refugees,
            military personnel,
            and others.
19 In carrying out their duties,
    bishops are free to operate without hindrance
    from civil authorities.
20 Bishops are to be appointed by the Church,
    not by civil rulers,
    and we ask those civil rulers who hold this right,
    or have received it through custom or treaty,
        to voluntarily end the practice.
21 We urge bishops to resign
    who find the discharge of their duties
    a burden because of illness or age.
        Provision will be made for their care
        or for special rights they deserve.

2. Diocesan Boundaries

22 In order for a diocese to serve the Gospel
    its people must understand the nature of the Church
    and the bishop be able to be effective among them.
One of the factors that will serve this well
    is the diocesan boundary,

and as a means of improving certain boundaries,
    we decree that a fitting revision
    take place as soon as possible.
This mandate can be met by revision of current boundaries,
    dismembering dioceses,
    uniting dioceses,
    moving the see city,
    or reorganizing the internal structure.
23 In doing this, the first concern
    is to provide each diocese with internal unity
        and continuous territory.
Organizers should keep in mind
    the need for pastoral offices,
    civil jurisdictions,
    and population centers.
The size of each diocese should be such
    that a bishop can know the priests and people
    and can carry out his duties well.
And each diocese should have sufficient clergy
    and other ministry specialists on staff
    to adequately meet the local needs.
And, where a sizable number of people live
    who are of an Eastern Church
    or of a different language group,
    provision should be made for their needs.
24 If diocesan boundaries are revised in such a way
    that Eastern Churches are affected,
    planning should be done with the Roman Curia.

3. Those Who Cooperate with the Diocesan Bishop in His Pastoral Task

25 The welfare of the flock of Christ
    is the primary concern

whenever we discuss the office of bishop.
Often it is necessary to appoint auxiliary bishops
    in order to insure this welfare,
    and sometimes coadjutor bishops are even needed.
In both cases, the appointed helper bishop
    is to be of one mind with the diocesan bishop
    and should be obedient to him in all matters.
26 Bishops should not hesitate to ask for these appointments,
    and even when they are not allowed,
    the bishops can and should appoint other clergy
        to leadership roles.

27 A diocesan vicar general is the most important office
    in the diocesan Curia,
    but a bishop may also appoint episcopal vicars
    to stand in his place around the diocese.
Those serving on the priests' senate also contribute
    to the bishop's work.
All priests and laypeople working in diocesan jobs
    should understand that they are assisting the bishop.
We strongly urge that a pastoral council be formed
    in every diocese as well,
    which would include clergy, religious, and laity
    and which would investigate and weigh matters
        that bear on pastoral activity.
28 All priests of a diocese
    share one priesthood with the bishop,
    who has the freedom and power
    to assign offices and pastorates.
The bishop is to consult with his priests
    about pastoral matters at regular intervals,
    and the priests are to contribute to the welfare
        of the whole diocese.
29 Those priests engaged in diocesan work

make a special contribution.

30 Parish priests have an important role,
  however, in the immediate needs of the people.
Parish priests are to carry out their pastoral work
  in such a way that the people really feel
  they are part of the diocese itself.
Moreover, priests should reach out to those
  who are not yet members of the Church
    to welcome them.
Community living for priests is strongly encouraged
  to make this reality possible.
Pastors are to preach the Gospel
  and offer catechetical instruction to all,
  working with trained religious and laypeople.
The celebration of the Eucharist
  is to be the center of parish life,
  along with the other sacraments,
    especially penance.
Pastors are to know their own people well,
  visiting homes and schools
  and paying special attention to the youth.
They are to devote themselves to the care of the poor,
  the ill,
  and working people.
Assistant pastors should be in fraternal union
  with their pastors.

31 In making pastoral appointments,
  bishops should consider a priest's suitability
  because the parish exists solely for the care of souls.
Pastors should have relative stability in their assignments,
  and although the bishop may move them,
  the process of determining this is to be simplified.
We urge pastors to resign voluntarily
  who are too old or ill to discharge their duties.

32 Concern for souls is also the criterion to use
   when opening or closing parishes.

33 Religious men and women
      (all those who take the vows)
      also contribute to the local Church
      through prayer,
            works of penance,
            and the example of their lives.
We hope they will also enter vigorously into
      the diocesan apostolate.
34 Religious priests can be said to "belong" to the clergy
      of the diocese in which they live,
      and other members of religious communities
            can also be said to "belong" to the diocese.
35 In order to ensure harmony in a diocese,
      religious women and men should pay attention
      to the bishop and help when called upon to do so.
Keeping within the mission of their own calling,
      religious should eagerly accept duties in the diocese
            and, unless they are contemplative,
            should adapt their own constitutions
            to allow for this, if they do not now.
But bishops should also allow religious
      to be faithful to the rule of their communities.
Certain communities are exempt from this
      and are under the authority of the pope
      for the good of the universal Church.
But all religious, whether exempt or not,
      must follow diocesan rules when working there,
      especially regarding Liturgy,
            formation,
            and the care of souls.
Schools conducted by religious fall under the authority

of the local bishop
as well as other matters of dress and conduct.
We call for a high level of mutual cooperation
among bishops and religious superiors
springing from a supernatural attitude of mind.

Chapter Three
CONCERNING THE COOPERATION OF BISHOPS FOR THE
COMMON GOOD OF MANY CHURCHES

1. Synods, Councils, and Especially Episcopal Conferences

36 Taking their lead from the apostles
who shared a common life together
and met to decide the welfare of the early Church,
this council ardently wants such meetings to flourish
to meet today's needs more adequately.
37 We believe the mission of the Church
cannot be advanced
unless bishops work together,
and, therefore, we consider it important
that bishops in nations or regions
form associations and meet together,
and do so often!
38 An episcopal conference is a council
in which bishops of a nation gather
to set programs that benefit the whole country.
Members include all local diocesan bishops of every rite,
coadjutors, auxiliaries, and titular bishops,
but not vicars general.

Each conference should have statutes
    establishing a board,
    a secretariat,
    and local rules about who can vote.
Conference decisions are binding
    when they result from deliberations and voting
    with two-thirds majority under its rules
    and when that decision has been approved
        by the pope.

2. The Boundaries of Ecclesiastical Provinces and the Establishment of Ecclesiastical Regions

[39] The welfare of souls suggests some revision
    in the current system of gathering dioceses together
    in local groups within nations.
[40] Therefore, a worldwide review of provinces and regions
    is to be undertaken
    with an eye to better organization.
[41] Local bishops should undertake this review
    and submit their suggestions to the pope.

3. Bishops with an Interdiocesan Office

[42] Certain functions in the Church will unfold better
    if they are shared among dioceses,
    and we recommend that regions or nations
        proceed to establish such offices.
[43] Every nation should have a military vicar
    to coordinate the special needs for those people.
Diocesan bishops should allow sufficient priests
    to carry out military pastoral work.

General Directive

44 We hereby direct that,
    when the code of canon law is revised
    laws should be written to implement this decree.
We also order that general directories be drawn up
    concerning the care of souls
    for use by both bishops and pastors,
    including groups with special needs.
Likewise, a catechetical directory should be composed
    dealing with fundamental principles
    and the preparation of books for that purpose.

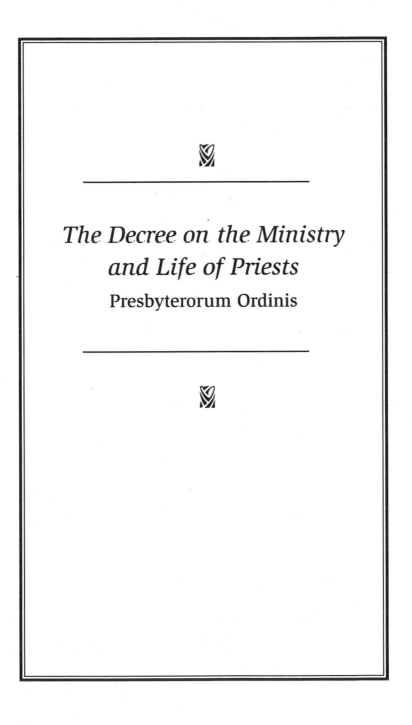

The Decree on the Ministry and Life of Priests

Presbyterorum Ordinis

Chapter Seven

⊗

PART ONE: BACKGROUND

*T*his document has its origins in the second session of Vatican II when, during a discussion on the constitution on the Church, some council fathers called for a fuller treatment of the priesthood. During that session, in fact, a trial balloon was circulated on this matter, a "message to priests." But the council saw this as inadequate compared to the rather extensive work being done on the Church's understanding of the roles of the bishops and the laity.

On October 13, 1964, during the third session of the council, debate opened on the council floor on a series of propositions outlining in rather brief form the major principles governing the Church's regard for its priests. Once again, the council fathers were not pleased and called for a more extensive treatment. (A principal speaker on this topic at that time was Cardinal Albert Meyer of Chicago.)

On October 19, 1964, the council sent the propositions back to commission for further revision and a full decree on the life and ministry of priests in the modern Church.

During the fourth session of Vatican II, a full year later, the commission resubmitted the document. The council fathers found this third version much more to their liking. But, at this same time, word began to spread among the council fathers that some of them would introduce a debate on the continuation of priestly celibacy as it is practiced in the Western (or Latin Rite) Church. (Note that the Eastern Churches in union with the pope do not require the discipline of celibacy for their priests.)

On the evening of October 10, 1965, some of the more conservative cardinals dined privately with Pope Paul VI and convinced him to prevent this debate on celibacy. On the following morning, the president of the day read to the council assembly a letter from the pope. In this letter, Pope Paul VI said that he did not wish to infringe on the right of any fathers to express themselves but that he did not think this an opportune moment to discuss celibacy because of its great importance and sensitivity.

The pope went on to say that he fully intended to maintain this "ancient, holy, and providential law" and that if any council father wished to speak about the matter he should do so in writing and should submit the letter to the council president, who would, in turn, pass it on to him.

In the end, the debate on the *Decree on the Ministry and Life of Priests* occurred without considering celibacy. Most of the council fathers applauded the pope's position.

The council approved the document by a vote of 2,390 to 4, and the pope promulgated it on December 7, 1965. The main contribution of the *Decree on the Ministry and Life of Priests* is that it corrects a pre-Vatican II mind-set that the priest is a "cult figure," somehow separated from the rest of the faithful. The document says, instead, that priests are drawn from among the people and are consecrated by the Holy Spirit, changed to become like Christ in the very depths of their beings.

The document clearly states that the priest is called to "service." He is to remain a human being, to remain part of the faithful of the Church. The bishop, not the priest, possesses the fullness of holy orders. Some but not all of the bishop's powers are delegated to priests. But in all cases, it is a power to serve, not to dominate.

Over and over again, the document reminds us that the center of Christian life, of parish life, and therefore of the life of the priest is the Eucharist. The *Decree on the Ministry and Life of Priests* develops the theme that priests move into holiness when they do their work, which is to say, when they make present the Eucharist.

PART TWO: PARAPHRASE TEXT

*F*rom the Vatican II document promulgated on December 7, 1965

Introduction

1 Because ministries of increasing difficulty
    are being assigned to priests
    in today's Church,
    we wish to provide a full treatment
        of their ministry and life.
Priests share in the work of Christ,
    who was the Teacher,
    the priestly minister,
    and the Servant Ruler.
They are responsible for the Church:
    the People of God,
    the Body of Christ,
    and the temple of the Holy Spirit.
Because all this is so,

and because their situations
in the Church and the world
have changed so dramatically,
     we issue this decree.

Chapter One
THE PRIESTHOOD IN THE MISSION OF THE CHURCH

2 Jesus Christ is the Anointed One!
   The very name *Christ* means just that:
   "the one anointed for service."
Christ has likewise shared his anointing
   through the Spirit with all the faithful,
   making us all a holy and royal priesthood.
In short, we are all anointed just as Christ was.

Hence, every member of the Church is called
   to offer spiritual sacrifices to God,
   to proclaim the wonders of God's love,
   to announce the end of darkness
       and the dawn of the age of Christ.
Each member of the Church is called for this work!

And the same Christ also established certain specific roles
   through which some people are called
   to provide for the public needs of the community.
Paul pointed out in his Letter to the Romans
   that not all the members of the Church
   have the same function and role.
Certain ones, therefore, are assigned the public task
   of presiding at Mass and the sacrament of penance
       among other sacred moments.

Christ sent his apostles out to minister
    just as he himself had been sent by God.
The successors of the apostles, who are today's bishops,
    likewise send others out to the vineyard
    just as they have been sent by Christ.

The bishops, in turn, send priests into their ministry
    as coworkers to continue Christ's work.
By a special sacrament, the ones chosen are anointed
    for the work of the priesthood
    and can act in the person of Christ.
God, likewise, gives priests the grace
    to provide the rest of the faithful
    with its spiritual needs,
        especially through the Eucharist.
The power and force of the priesthood
    is derived from the Gospel
    and the life, death, and resurrection of Christ.
The purpose of the work of priests, therefore,
    is that God be glorified through Christ,
    which is to say
        that people come to believe in Christ
        with freedom, knowledge, and gratitude.
Everything a priest does is directed toward this:
    that people come to Christ,
    which is how God receives honor.

3 Now priests, of course,
    are chosen from the human family
    in order to serve that family
    just as Christ did.
While they are set apart a bit in the human family,
    this is in order that they can be dedicated
        entirely,

wholly,
and completely to God.
They cannot serve God without being in touch
with the divine life,
and they cannot serve people without being in touch
with human life.
They are in the world but not *of* the world,
working as shepherds among their flocks.
The virtues that support this work
are goodness of heart;
sincerity and strength;
depth of personality;
a faithful pursuit of justice;
a civil tongue;
and a dedication to truth,
beauty,
and love.

Chapter Two
THE MINISTRY OF PRIESTS

Part One: Priestly Functions

4 The first and foremost duty of priests
is to proclaim the Word of God,
which, for most people,
is their first point of contact
with matters of faith.
This is often a difficult task in today's world.
In announcing the Good News
and proclaiming the Word,
care should be taken that it be done in terms

that today's people understand
and can apply to their lives.
Preaching of this sort is especially necessary
    for the presentation of the sacraments,
    in particular the Liturgy of the Word.
The sacraments, after all, are born of the Word.

5 Priests are also consecrated to perform
    certain sacred functions in the community.
First, they normally preside at the sacraments,
    including baptism and the sacrament of penance
    in addition to the anointing of the sick and dying.

Second, the Eucharist is central in the ministry of priests.
    It is the source of all Christian life
    and the summit of all Christian work.
It is, in short, the very heartbeat of every parish,
    and priests should take their role in it
        with great sincerity.
They should teach the rest of the faithful
    how to participate fully in the Liturgy
    and they should offer their lives together with them
        at Mass.

Third, they are called to recite the divine office,
    and by doing so, they extend themselves
    into each hour of each day
    and pray on behalf of all.
And fourth, they maintain the parish church,
    keeping it in order
    and ensuring that it is always a place of prayer.

6 The priest is, furthermore, the leader of his parish
    in the name of the local bishop

and has a certain spiritual power for this work.
His role is to teach and, sometimes, to correct people
    and to present the Christian doctrine
    with clarity and force.
Toward this end, he is a teacher of "the Faith."

He teaches by how he lives
    and by how he presides at the rites,
        as well as by his words.
He has a special duty to assist the weak
    in their faith
    and to provide for young people,
        married people,
        parents,
        the sick and dying,
        and men and women religious.
Priests have a special and unique obligation
    to assist the poor and lowly,
    as Christ himself did.
The priest's task is to promote a communal life,
    not merely individually faithful people,
    and the center of that life is, again,
        the Eucharist.
As we have said already,
    the Eucharist is where the Christian life originates,
    and communities themselves, as the Body of Christ,
        must be charitable,
            missionary in spirit,
            prayerful,
            and faithful.
The priest, therefore, must never become ideological
    but must adhere only to the Gospel.

Part Two: Priests As Related to Others

7 Priests and bishops relate very closely
    and form one unit.
They occasionally express this through concelebration,
    but every time the Mass is celebrated,
    the bishop is symbolically present in the priest
    as a sign of the presence of Christ.
The bishop, for his part,
    must regard priests as brothers and friends,
    caring for their spiritual and material needs
        and in particular for their holiness.
He should have a role like a father or a counselor
    to his priests, allowing them to speak
    and hearing them out on important matters.
A "senate of priests" can advance this goal.
And priests, likewise, must stand by their bishops,
    cooperating with them and working together
    to build up the Church,
        for no priest operates alone.

8 No matter what their specific role in the Church,
    priests form one brotherhood
    and are bound to support one another.
Their roles vary:
    parish ministry,
    teaching and research,
    manual labor among the workers of the world,
    or other apostolic tasks.
But they still form a single, united priesthood,
    sharing a bond of charity.
Experienced priests should offer newly ordained ones
    a helping hand
    and be understanding

about their new ways of thinking.
Newly ordained priests should respect the wisdom
    of those who are their seniors.
As much as possible, priests should share a communal life,
    offering each other support and comfort
    and paying special attention to their brothers
        who have personal difficulties.

9 Priests are also among the baptized
    and take their place in the Family of God
    as members of that family among other members.
All who are in the Body of Christ
    have passed through the waters of baptism
    and all share in the life of Christ, including priests.
Therefore, when they preside at prayer
    or over the life of the parish,
    priests should be certain that it is Christ's will,
        not their own,
        which is being accomplished.
Toward this end, they must work
    with the rest of the faithful
    promoting the dignity of the laypeople
    and supporting their role in the Gospel's work.

They should listen to the laity
    with a willing spirit
    and accept their competence,
        trusting them to know the modern times.
Priests stand among the laity
    to serve them as leaders
    and to bring holy order into the life of the Church.
As such, they should accept the gifts of laypeople
    and allow them to minister side by side,
    even working on their own initiative sometimes.

As leaders, priests must reconcile differences
    yet alienate no one,
        defend the common good
        yet protect the faith,
            welcoming all to Christ.
And laypeople, for their part,
    must love and support their priests,
    treating them as shepherds and fathers,
        working faithfully with them.

Part Three: The Distribution of Priests and Priestly Vocations

10 The priesthood of Christ
    is meant for all people everywhere,
    and priests, therefore, serve the world.
There are no limits on who is served—
    neither race nor nationality,
    neither age nor status.
The rules in the Church that govern
    how priests are assigned
    and under which bishop they serve
        should be revised with an eye
        to their worldwide mission.
The needs of the whole world should be considered
    in deciding where priests will serve,
    and national boundaries should be ignored.
As much as possible,
    when priests are sent out to a mission site,
    they should have companions,
        and care should be taken
        to ensure their mental and spiritual health.
And priests sent to such work
    should learn the local language and customs

to be better able to serve well.

11 All the Christian faithful,
and especially priests,
should foster priestly vocations
and help those who express an interest in them.

Chapter Three
THE LIFE OF PRIESTS

Part One: The Priestly Call to Perfection

12 All the Christian people
are called to grow more perfectly
into the image of Christ.
Priests have a special obligation to attend to this growth
for themselves and for their brothers
because of their role as presider and leader
among the rest of the faithful.
Priests, after all, represent the person of Christ
and receive a special grace
to work among God's people.
This special grace allows them to live without
the pleasures of the flesh
and with full dedication to service.
God can work through anyone,
even an unworthy minister,
but God normally chooses those
found to be holy
and close to God.
This council urges all priests, therefore,
to grow in sanctity.

13 And, in fact, the way for a priest to grow in holiness
    is to work in priestly labors.
They should be ready to receive the Word
    which they proclaim
    and to be like Christ
        to whom they witness.
And by ridding themselves of sexual desire
    and evil habits,
        priests more faithfully serve Christ.

Priests are strongly encouraged to celebrate Mass
    each and every day,
        uniting their whole selves to Christ.
They are encouraged to be ready to offer penance
    whenever someone asks,
    to pray the divine office,
    and even to lay down their lives, if necessary.
They are encouraged to console the distressed
    and to teach those who ask,
    to govern their communities with fairness,
    and to pastor the souls of the rest of the faithful,
        whether convenient for them or not.

14 Above all, priests should strive to unify
    their interior spiritual and emotional lives
    with their exterior program of pastoral work.
By uniting themselves with Christ,
    who is united to God,
    priests can accomplish this inner unity
        which will produce great fruit
        for the "Gospel."
The eucharistic meal is the place wherein this happens
    most readily.
By offering themselves each time they preside,

priests will come more and more to resemble Christ,
who likewise offered himself to us.
Conformity to the laws of the Church and the bishops
is part of this for the priest,
since it is the same as loyalty toward Christ
and results in interior peace and unity.

Part Two: Special Spiritual Needs of Priestly Life

15 Priests must strive to do the work of Christ
and not to seek their own will.
In practice, this means priests must develop obedience
to their bishops or other superiors
who speak in the name of Christ.
They ought to gladly allow themselves to be spent
performing those duties assigned to them
and pouring themselves out in service.
Such obedience to superiors produces unity
within the Church
and allows priests to set their sights on ministry.
In their work, priests should seek new ways
to announce the Gospel,
humbly present their new ideas to their bishops,
and obediently accept the bishop's decision.
By such an approach, priests become like Christ
who "obediently accepted death on a cross."

16 Priests of the Western Church are also called
to embrace celibacy
for the sake of the Reign of God.
Indeed, celibacy is not demanded
by the nature of the priesthood itself,
which is clear because the Eastern Churches
do not practice it.

And while we do not intend to change the Eastern custom,
we do intend to maintain celibacy
in the Western Church.
We believe this serves the Church best
because it makes the priest available,
ready,
and undivided in his heart.
We think of celibacy as a gift to the Church,
and we exhort all who have accepted it
to remain faithful to it.

17 Priests are also called to develop
a proper relationship to material possessions
and to embrace voluntary poverty.
The values they cultivate regarding such things
can render them free for service
and make them an example of freedom to others.
They are to use the goods of this world
for God's work
and reject every other use.
With the help of trained laypeople,
priests should administer the materialities
of their parishes in similar fashion.
These, too, should be directed toward God's work
and nothing else.
They should provide for the cost of divine worship,
an honest salary for the clergy,
the pastoral work of the Church,
and the needs of the poor and needy.
Priests should not derive a financial profit
from their pastoral assignment
and should never set their hearts on riches.
By sharing things in common, priests can live
according to the poverty of Christ,

and can better serve the poor.
The home of the priest should be utterly approachable
by everyone, even the most humble person.

Part Three: The Means of Support for Priestly Life

[18] Priests have both ancient and modern tools
which God's Spirit gives to all
to foster a more deeply spiritual life.
They have, first and foremost,
the Scriptures and the Eucharist.
They have, as well, the rest of the sacraments;
spiritual reading;
a devotion to Mary;
daily prayer, especially with Christ in the Eucharist;
regular retreats;
and professional spiritual direction.

[19] Priests must also be fully knowledgeable
about Church doctrine and dogma:
the teachings of the popes,
church councils,
the ancient Mothers and Fathers,
the magisterium,
and theologians.

They should also be aware of the issues of today:
those things that are on people's minds
as they come to the Church for guidance.
Toward this end, institutes should be established
and continuing education programs fostered.
Bishops should make it easier for pastors
to obtain formation in pastoral ministry,
theology,

and spirituality.
Some priests should be allowed to become professional
   in their work with theology and spirituality.

20 Priests should be paid a fair salary,
   and the rest of the faithful are bound to provide it.
Bishops are to see that this happens
   and also to fairly compensate others
   who may also serve alongside the priest
      or in support of him.
They should also be given annual vacations.
   The old system of benefices
   should be reformed.

21 In certain cases, bishops should organize
   a system of clerical financial support,
   and wealthier dioceses can help needy ones.
Laypeople can be employed to assist in this.
The retirement needs of priests
   and of those who serve with them
   should also be considered.
By providing for priests in this way,
   they will be more able to do their work
   without having to worry about their security.

Conclusion and Exhortation

22 We cannot overlook the difficulties
   that priests face today
   even though we know there are also joys.
Priests, like the laypeople in their parishes,
   must often feel almost like strangers in the world:

looking for meaning
and for ways to communicate.
But we should always remember
that God is with us;
we are not alone.
There are many gifts in the world,
many talents,
and each of them is a stone with which
to build the Church.
We will find new ways to announce the Gospel
because God is with us.

And not only that,
we are also with each other—
priests, laypeople, bishops—
forming one community,
supporting one another,
working together for God's Reign.

Little by little, that Reign of God
is established.
The leaders of the Church
must, therefore, walk by faith,
as did Abraham and Sarah.

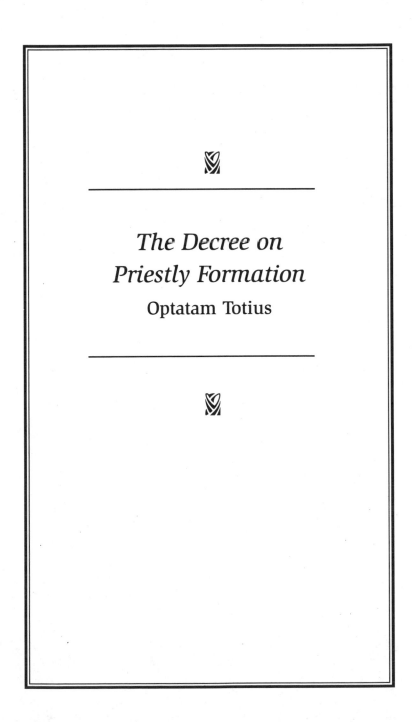

The Decree on Priestly Formation
Optatam Totius

Chapter Eight

⁂

PART ONE: BACKGROUND

*T*his document was not introduced for debate until November 12, 1964, but it was in preparation throughout the council's proceedings. One reads in it a great fidelity to the *Dogmatic Constitution on the Church*, the foundational document of Vatican II. The *Decree on Priestly Formation* names the mystery of the Church articulated in the constitution as the basis of theological and pastoral training for priests.

The decree also pays attention to the *Pastoral Constitution on the Church in the Modern World* and the *Constitution on the Sacred Liturgy* and, indeed, cannot be read separately from them.

Coming as it did toward the end of the council was appropriate for a practical document such as this one which seeks to implement the spirit and theology of the council. From its introduction to the final vote, this decree was found widely acceptable with only a few suggestions for amendment, mainly from those who wished to reduce the exclusivity of Thomism in seminary training.

The council fathers approved the decree on October 28, 1965, by a vote of 2,318 to 3.

PART TWO: PARAPHRASE TEXT

*F*rom the Vatican II document
promulgated on October 28, 1965

Preface

1 We bishops working here at Vatican II
    for the renewal of the whole Church
    fully realize that such a renewal depends,
        in large part,
        on the ministry of priests
        animated by the Spirit of Christ.

Beginning with Jesus' words as he sent his apostles
    to carry his mission to the world
    and continuing through our history,
        the progress of the People of God
        has always depended on priests this way.
Therefore, we intend to articulate certain principles
    to provide guidance in the training of priests.
By doing this, we will implement the pronouncements
    of this council
    as well as better meet the demands of the times.

Chapter One
PROGRAM OF PRIESTLY FORMATION
TO BE UNDERTAKEN BY INDIVIDUAL COUNTRIES

Because of the diversity in the Church
    around the world,

we can set only general guidelines here.
Therefore, each nation or rite
     should develop a well-defined program
     for priestly formation.
This program should be prepared by the bishops,
     revised from time to time,
     and approved by the pope.
Universal norms should be adapted in these programs
     in order to meet the local pastoral needs.

Chapter Two
THE INTENSIFIED ENCOURAGEMENT OF PRIESTLY VOCATIONS

2 The entire world needs more vocations today;
     it is one of the greatest challenges
     faced by today's Church.
The whole Christian community is responsible
     for encouraging vocations to the priesthood,
     and the principal way that is done
          is by living as solid Christians.
Families alive with the Spirit of God
     can help with this,
     and likewise parishes whose vigorous vitality
          attracts and sustains young people.
Teachers and others associated with young men
     can help them hear God's call
     as can every priest whose very life
          is a model for others.
Bishops, too, have a role in promoting vocations
     and should guide those who may be called.
By partnering in this way,
     the People of God will assist the Holy Spirit

to prompt those properly suited for this work
    to step forward.
Steadfast prayer is the basis of this work,
    along with penance and preaching
    working side by side with well-planned campaigns
        to attract and foster vocations.
[3] Minor seminaries provide fertile ground
    in which the seeds of a vocation can grow.
They should be operated in such a way
    that the age of the candidate is considered
    and that social,
        cultural,
        and family contacts
            can be maintained.
Programs for those entering the seminary as adults
    should also be available.

Chapter Three
THE PROGRAMMING OF MAJOR SEMINARIES

[4] There is no doubt
    that major seminaries are necessary
    to prepare men for the priesthood
    because this is where students are prepared
        to care for the souls of the faithful,
        following the example of Christ.
Candidates for the priesthood should be prepared
    to undertake a ministry of Word,
    understanding Scripture,
        living by it,
        and preaching it.
They should likewise be ready

to undertake a ministry of worship,
presiding at sacred liturgies,
especially the Eucharist.

And they should also be trained
to undertake the ministry of the pastor,
serving the People of God
in both administration
and programs of pastoral care.
Every training program should meet these goals,
offer practical implementation,
and come under the authority of the bishop.

5 Because the seminary is the heart of the diocese
and because those trained there
learn from example as well as instruction,
the greatest care should be taken to be certain
that those selected as seminary staff
can model priestly life well.
Faculty and formation personnel should be chosen
from among the best in the diocese
and carefully prepared for their work,
both through experience
and their own doctrinal training.
Together with the rector, the students, and the local bishop,
the seminary community
should be like a united family.

6 Careful judgment should be made
about the fitness of candidates
and their freedom of choice.
The highest standards should be maintained,
regardless of the need for priests,
trusting that God will provide for the Church.

7 Where appropriate, several dioceses may cooperate
in operating major seminaries.

Chapter Four
THE DEEPENING OF SPIRITUAL FORMATION

8 Seminary programs should combine spiritual formation
with instruction and pastoral training
and make use of spiritual directors
to guide this for each student.
Students should be encouraged to a personal piety
in keeping with the customs of the Church
though they should be careful that their formation
not consist solely of such piety
which may produce
unsubstantial religious feelings.
They should, rather,
be molded in the likeness of Christ,
finding Christ everywhere:
in meditation,
through active use of the sacraments,
during the praying of the divine office,
in obedience to their bishops,
and in the parish to which they are assigned.
9 Those preparing for priesthood
should be deeply saturated by the mystery
which is the Church,
especially as restated in this council.
This means they will live the Paschal Mystery
in their own lives,
giving themselves to service
rather than expecting honor

or dominating their flock.
Theirs should be a life of humble living
　　and self-denial.
In their preparation, they should be made fully aware
　　of the obligations they would accept if ordained.
10 If the rite in which they are ordained requires it,
　　students should be prepared for celibacy
　　　　through which they renounce the companionship
　　　　　　that marriage provides most people.
Through celibacy, they can devote themselves to God
　　with an undivided love,
　　witnessing to life in the world to come
　　and becoming all things to all people.
They should see celibacy as a gift
　　and undertake it freely,
　　　　forewarned of the threat of modern society
　　　　　to such a choice
　　　　and aided by both human and divine help.
11 Seminary programs should be developed
　　on the basis of sound psychology and pedagogy,
　　developing stable human maturity
　　　　in the candidates:
　　　　　　emotional stability,
　　　　　　ability to make decisions,
　　　　　　and fairness in judging others.
They should grow to be sincere of heart,
　　constantly concerned for justice,
　　faithful to their word,
　　courteous in manner and speech.
And their training should be based on discipline
　　which leads them to self-mastery
　　and the ability to grow internally
　　　　and govern themselves.
12 Bishops may ask students to undertake internships

during their training
or as transitional deacons.

Chapter Five
THE REVISION OF ECCLESIASTICAL STUDIES

13 Seminarians should be equipped for advanced study
    with thorough training in human and social sciences
    appropriate to their own culture and nation.
They should also have a command of Latin
    and other languages necessary to study
        both Scripture and tradition.

14 In revising seminary programs,
    the first goal should be
    to integrate theology with philosophy,
    which flow together in understanding the mystery
        that is Christ and the Church.

15 The study of philosophy leads students
    to a deep understanding of the world,
        humankind,
        and God.
Students should know about modern trends
    and current scientific programs
    so they can engage the people of today
        in a meaningful way.
This will also enable students to recognize the truth
    and detect error.
Furthermore, by developing a method of teaching
    that enables students to love their studies
    and cherish the truth they discover,

seminarians will gain deeper insight
into the mysteries of faith.

16 The study of theology has sacred Scripture
    as its soul.
Seminarians are to be trained well
    in modern methods of understanding Scripture
    and learn to make it the soul
        of their own spirituality as well!
In teaching dogma, biblical themes should be taught first,
    followed by our own ancient writers
    and the general history of the Church.
Students should then be thoroughly familiar
    with the work of Thomas Aquinas
    and other Doctors of the Church
    and consider how the mysteries of faith
        can be communicated effectively
        to modern women and men.
Moral theology should also be taught,
    based again on Scripture.
When teaching canon law to seminarians,
    the mystery of the Church should be foremost
    as it is explained by this council.
And, of course, sacred Liturgy,
    the primary source of life for the faithful,
    should be taught everywhere faithfully.
Students should also be taught courses
    about those Churches with whom we are not united
    so they can assist with the restoration of unity.

17 Teaching methods are to be revised in such a way
    that theology is integrated into the very life
        of the seminarian
        and does not remain mere information.

Excessive class work should be replaced with formation.
[18] Those men suited for it
    should be sent to advanced training
    so the Church will have enough scholars.

Chapter Six
THE PROMOTION OF STRICTLY PASTORAL TRAINING

[19] Seminarians should be especially well trained
    in the art of caring for souls:
        in catechetics,
        in preaching skills,
        in sacramental and liturgical presiding,
        in works of charity,
        in evangelization,
        and in other pastoral skills.
In general, priests should be trained
    to dialogue openly with others,
    to listen to others' concerns,
    and to reveal their hearts in a spirit of charity.
[20] Seminarians should learn to make use of modern methods
    of teaching, healing, and counseling.
They should encourage laypeople to their own work
    and keep in mind the needs
    of the whole Church.
[21] Toward this end, students should participate in courses
    that offer practical training and internships
    under the guidance of well-trained supervisors.

Chapter Seven
THE REFINEMENT OF TRAINING AFTER THE COURSE OF STUDIES

22 Once ordained, priests should continue to study
because of constantly advancing knowledge
combined with the changing needs of modern times.
Programs to assist them in this should be established
so younger priests will be properly integrated.

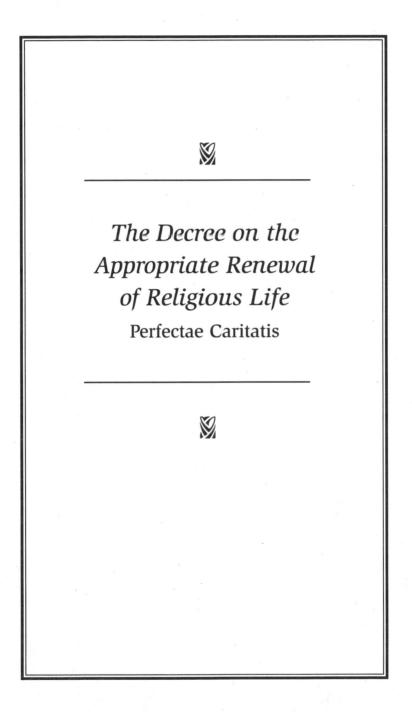

The Decree on the Appropriate Renewal of Religious Life

Perfectae Caritatis

Chapter Nine

※

PART ONE: BACKGROUND

*T*his document, like others, elaborates themes first discussed in the *Dogmatic Constitution on the Church*. Knowing that the renewal of the Church would depend upon a corresponding renewal of the Church's religious men and women, the council addressed itself here to that matter.

When the first schema of this document was introduced for debate on November 10, 1964, the council fathers found the treatment too narrow. They wanted a more wide-ranging reform of religious life, especially where an overly rigorous lifestyle conflicted with the active work of members. The council fathers expressed a general desire that religious, especially sisters and nuns, be treated as adults rather than as "children," which many communities seemed to do through systems of arbitrary punishment and assignment.

A call was sounded that mother superiors be less "maternal" and abandon customs that made their members feel infantile or inferior. The need was seen to address the style of habits worn, especially by women religious, and, in general, to update their rule of life to more suitably address the needs of today's Church.

Among the difficulties cited in the first text considered by the council was the fact that it had been drawn up entirely by men, without any formal consultation with the women who would be greatly affected by it.

Sister Mary Luke Tobin, of the Sisters of Loretto, who had been appointed an auditor, called for a better document, one that would express a theology consistent with the *aggiornamento* of the whole council and one that would provide for women religious to serve on the church bodies that govern them.

In the end, the progressives succeeded in sending the schema into major revisions based on hundreds of suggested amendments from the floor.

When the final document came into the council for debate and approval, it did not include any major improvements over the first draft. The commission that prepared it, headed by the extremely conservative Cardinal Antoniutti of the Roman Curia, refused to see any call for change in terms other than "disobedient rebellion."

No women religious were included in the deliberations of the commission. The result was that the call for reform was largely concerned with external matters: garb, lifestyle, rule, and so forth. The document did not enter into an extensive theological reflection on the role and place of religious life in today's Church. In the end, whatever deeper reform would occur would be in the hands of religious men and women themselves.

And, indeed, renewal of religious life in modern times did not begin nor did it end at the Second Vatican Council. Even before the council began, a well-developed movement among religious was already sweeping through the Church, including a movement to change the style of the garb.

The progressive forces of Vatican II allowed a less fully developed document to emerge from the council, perhaps, for three reasons: First, they knew that men and women religious would take up this cause after the council as they already had before it. Second, they had many other major tasks on their hands in the fourth session. Third, they had really lost the theological battle on this issue much earlier, and moving the implacable Cardinal Antoniutti would have been extremely difficult.

The council fathers approved the *Decree on the Appropriate Renewal of Religious Life* by a vote of 2,321 to 4, and the pope promulgated it on October 28, 1965.

One of the outstanding features of this document occurs in its first few articles. These outline a method for reform. No other council document so explicitly describes a method. Prior to Vatican II, no serious reform of the Church had been undertaken for many, many centuries, so there existed no real method for deciding on reform and enacting it. But this document clearly roots all reform in the Scriptures and in the spirit of "the founders." The decree then suggests that current structures, rules, and customs be updated to meet the demands of the day. In a nutshell, this is the method the council used throughout its work on all other issues as well.

PART TWO: PARAPHRASE TEXT

*F*rom the Vatican II document
promulgated on October 28, 1965

1 We bishops of the world
    have already said
    (in the *Dogmatic Constitution on the Church*)
    that the vowed, religious life
        flows from Christ.
Now we want to give some general principles
    by which religious orders of women and men

can renew themselves to meet their own needs
and better serve the Church in these times.
From the beginning of Christianity,
certain men and women have emerged
who wished to live in complete dedication
to Christ.
They formed a network of religious communities,
wonderful and varied,
throughout the Church
and across the face of the earth.
Their presence in the Church has been essential
in the building up of the Reign of God,
and it is still essential today,
which is why we call for their renewal
along with the rest of the Church.

2 The method of their renewal
will follow two steps,
implemented under five principles:
First, they should return to the sources
of all Christian life
and to the original desires of their founders.
Second, they should adjust the community
to meet the conditions of today.
The renewal we seek should go forward, then,
under these principles:
First, the purpose and reason for religious life
is to more closely follow Christ
as his story is told in the Gospels.
Second, each community should understand
its own unique contribution to the Church
as that is rooted in its customs and in the spirit
of the ones who founded it.

Third, all religious communities should contribute
    to the greater Church,
    taking up needs in the apostolate such as
        the study of Scripture,
        the development of Liturgy,
        the teaching of doctrine,
        the work of pastors,
        the call to ecumenism,
        the needs of the missions,
        or works of charity and justice.
Fourth, all communities should promote
    among their members
    a keen awareness of the human conditions
        in today's world
        so that they might more adequately serve.
Fifth, because it is true that the goal of religious life
    is to lead us to Christ through the vows,
    communities must honestly come to terms
        with the fact
        that all the external changes in the world
        mean nothing unless there is likewise
            an interior renewal of heart
            which is first and foremost our goal.

3 Furthermore, the lifestyle of religious men and women
    should also be corrected where necessary
    so that it suits and serves the needs of their work,
        the local cultural customs,
        and social and economic realities.
The way in which these communities are governed
    should also be updated,
    and outmoded rules or customs
        should be ended at once.

4 This renewal cannot happen
     without the cooperation of all members
          of each community.
The responsibility for the renewal belongs to those
     who govern the communities,
     along with their general chapters,
     and each should follow its own path
          in deciding how renewal will occur.
Let us remember in this work
     that the hope of renewal
     lies in deep commitment to the spirit of the rule,
          not in the multiplication of laws.
5 Religious men and women, after all,
     are called to combine pious contemplation
     with zeal for apostolic works,
          remaining close to Christ in mind and heart
          while at the same time working hard
               for the Reign of God!
6 Therefore, religious communities should pray together
     and offer the Eucharist together daily
     so that, united at the table of Christ,
          they might have the grace for their work.
7 Those communities whose mission is strictly limited
     to contemplation, solitude, and silence
     should remain in their vocation,
          regardless of the demands of the times.
They should, however, also renew themselves
     according to these norms.
8 Those communities with active apostolates
     should also adjust their lifestyles and rules
     to fit these times more adequately.
Their renewal will vary according to their specific needs.
Their lifestyle should be penetrated
     by the Spirit of Christ

while their ministry is animated
    by God's presence.
9 The ancient and holy institution of monasticism
    should also be renewed
    while at the same time preserved.
10 The lay religious life also serves the Church
    in very important ways.
Such communities may call some to ordination
    to meet their own needs,
    provided they do not change their basic goals.
11 Likewise, secular institutes are to preserve
    their character and mission
    while at the same time providing
        for the spiritual needs of their members.

12 Here, now, are some reflections on the vows
    of celibacy, poverty, and obedience.

Celibacy should be seen as a gift of grace
    allowing those who follow it
    to burn with greater love for God
        and all humankind!
It is a way to access heavenly riches
    through the practice of mortification,
        which is "dying to one's self
        for the sake of others."
Just as Christ is the spouse of the Church,
    so those in vows of celibacy
    have a special union with God.
Those in vows and their superiors should remember
    that the current social trends
    argue against this choice.
Because of its inherent difficulties,
    this vow will be better lived

in the context of brotherly or sisterly love.
Only those people who have been tested
    and found suitably mature and ready
    should take this vow.

13 Poverty is another way for people
    to share in the life of Christ,
    who became poor for our sakes.
The poverty of which we speak
    is not the same as "destitution,"
    meaning that one should be poor in spirit,
        not merely in fact.

Those in a vow of poverty
    should work to provide for their means
    but should not have undue concern or anxiety
        for their welfare.
Communities should live as a witness to the world
    of a shared life,
    supporting the poor,
    showing love to all through hospitality,
    having only what they need to sustain themselves
        and nothing more.

14 Obedience is a third way
    for people to come close to Christ,
    who learned obedience through suffering.
Religious women and men become obedient
    to the Church and its needs
    by obeying their superiors
        based on their rule and constitution.
Those asked by a superior to undertake work
    should put their minds and hearts into it,
    and superiors, for their part,

should serve their companions
and operate with charity,
    prayerfulness,
    and fairness.
It is important that religious men and women
    be free to follow their consciences
    and have their personalities and talents
        taken into account
        when making assignments.
The working out of decisions about one's work
    should occur within a dialogue
    between superior and member
    while, in the end, the superior decides.

15 Religious communities should foster a common life,
    with brothers equal to priests in dignity,
    sisters equal to one another as well,
    and lay members equal to all others.
Except where diversity of works requires otherwise,
    all should be on the same level.
16 The papal cloister for nuns should be maintained
    but updated according to the wishes
    of the monasteries themselves.
17 Religious habits should be simple and modest,
    fitting into both the needs of the workplace
    as well as the health of the members.
They should be changed if they do not meet this norm.

18 Religious men and women should be properly trained
    for the work they undertake in the apostolate,
    which means they should not be arbitrarily assigned
        to apostolic work
        immediately after novitiate.
Rather, their religious and secular training

should both continue until they are truly ready.
Religious should be made aware of current cultural life—
    its manners, social customs, and lifestyles—
    so they can harmonize their work more evenly.
Those chosen as leaders should be carefully selected.

[19] New communities of religious should be founded
    only when the need for them is obvious,
    and thought should be given to the possibility
      that "fresh forms of religious life"
      might better serve the Church
      in certain situations.
[20] In order to continue to meet the needs of today's Church,
    religious communities should maintain their mission
      by developing new programs when needed
      and by abandoning what is no longer relevant.
[21] If it seems to the local bishop and the pope
    that certain communities have no hope of thriving,
    they should be prevented from accepting novices
    and possibly joined to other similar groups.
[22] Communities that are small,
    or that share a common mission with others,
    should consider joining forces through
      federations,
      associations,
      or mergers.

[23] The council affirms the formation
    of conferences of major superiors
    and suggests them as well for secular institutes.
[24] Vocations to religious life are sorely needed
    and should be fostered by parents,
      the communities themselves,
      and preaching.

25 This council has high regard for those called
    to live this life:
    virginal, poor, and obedient.
We know that Christ himself is the model.
We place great hope in you:
    in your labor,
    your prayers,
    and the unseen fruits of your lives!
May all religious men and women throughout the world
    spread the Gospel of Christ!

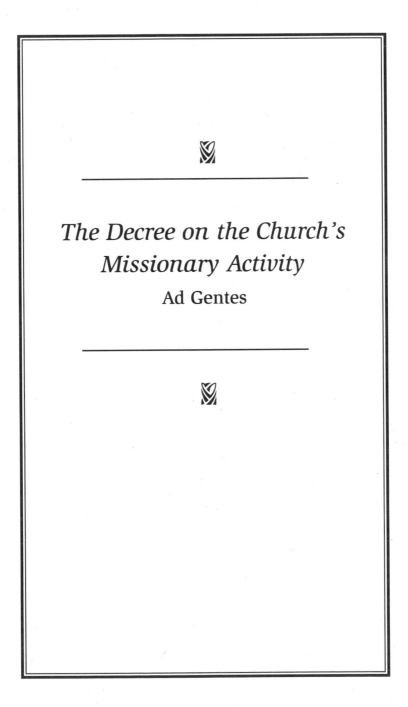

The Decree on the Church's Missionary Activity
Ad Gentes

Chapter Ten

※

PART ONE: BACKGROUND

*A*mong the major shifts in focus that occurred at Vatican II is the attitude of Catholic Christians toward other Christians and non-Christians. Specific documents address this shift (the *Decree on Ecumenism* and the *Declaration on the Relationship of the Church to Non-Christian Religions*) but the *Decree on the Church's Missionary Activity* builds yet another bridge.

The introduction of this document—on November 6, 1964, during the third session—was dramatic. On that particular day, Pope Paul VI, in a rare appearance, decided to attend an actual working session of the council. It is unclear why he chose to do this, but perhaps he wanted to underscore the newly defined sense of collegiality or to underline the fact that, ultimately, what came out of the council was his own prerogative. Whatever the reason, he chose November 6, 1964, and arrangements were hastily made for him to help introduce the first version of what later became the *Decree on the Church's Missionary Activity*.

On the word of a cardinal adviser, the pope spoke glowingly about the document and recommended it to the council fathers. Then he stood, blessed them gracefully, and left the council hall. As the debate proceeded over the next two and a half days, it became clear that the text as presented was not adequate, and the council fathers eventually sent the schema back to its commission for revisions, an embarrassment for the pope. The vote ran 1,601 to 311 in favor of revision.

The end of the third and the entire fourth session had tightly packed agendas, but because the council would clearly not continue past the fourth session, the schema on the Church's missionary activity was reintroduced on October 7, 1965, in a much fuller treatment than the former version.

A compromise document came out of the final discussion. Why? Partly because of the time schedule and partly because of the actions of nervous curial officials. Nonetheless, all the council fathers saw the theological development in chapter one of the document as a major move forward, and even though the final version did not address a number of issues on missionary activity, the council found the document, as a whole, acceptable.

The final vote on this document ran 2,394 to 5. The pope promulgated the *Decree on the Church's Missionary Activity* on December 7, 1965. It should be read in tandem with the above-mentioned documents on other Christians and non-Christians.

PART TWO: PARAPHRASE TEXT

*F*rom the Vatican II document
promulgated on December 7, 1965

Preface

[1] We in the Church have a strong sense
that we are called to offer all humans

that which makes human life most noble:
God's Word and presence!
We have a sense of mission about this
because of Christ's command
to preach the Gospel to all.
But this missionary self-identity also comes
from the nature of the Church itself:
that it is universal,
that is has something to offer to all,
that it addresses the entire world
with the Word of God.
We want to be the "salt of the earth"
and the "light of the world."
Now we wish to articulate how that will unfold
for the real benefit of all humankind
by setting down certain principles for this work.

Chapter One
DOCTRINAL PRINCIPLES

2 The Church is a pilgrim in this world
and, as we just said, by its very nature
seeks to make God's presence known
throughout the world.
This is the core of who the Church is:
it is "sent" to do Christ's work
and to be a "fountain of love" for all.
God's own generosity is expressed in this,
that all might become one family.

3 For the divine plan to bring all people
into wholeness and healing

is not a secret,
     nor found only within one's soul.
It is lived out in a much more public way
     in the continuing witness to Christ
     through whom God revealed Godself.
Jesus, human and divine,
     stood between light and darkness
     and opened the way of grace
          so all might be light.
That light,
     that en-*light*-enment
     that comes through Christ,
     provides a new human way of life:
          a life of grace and truth,
          a life of a shared divine nature,
          a life of being enriched by God,
          a life of service and love,
          a life, in short, of salvation!
How could we not desire in our deepest heart
     to share that with all the world?

4 In order to help us share that wonderful presence
     of the divine Spirit and life,
     we have received the Holy Spirit,
     who sealed us on Pentecost
          with this mission.
This Spirit gave us "one voice"
     for our work,
     making Christ's message understandable
          in every language
          and every culture of the world.
The Spirit now continues to give us the gifts
     that make missionary work possible:
          hierarchical order and leadership

and the gifts to preach and witness
as well as the desire to do so!
5 Jesus Christ was a truly powerful
and graceful person!
He laid the foundation of the Church
by calling followers to join with him
in living and witnessing to the truth.
The mission we now have is Christ's own:
to make disciples of all,
to baptize,
to teach God's way of life.
Since the time of Christ,
the duty to be missionaries
has indeed become ours as a Church.
We are present in the world through
our lifestyles,
our preaching,
our sacraments,
and in other ways as well.
To do this we must be like Christ:
poor;
obedient;
and willing to sacrifice everything,
sometimes even life itself,
for this cause!

6 The duty to be missionaries
falls mainly upon the bishops and the pope
with the prayers of the whole Church.
Little by little, the Word is spread
and new communities of Christians arise,
joining themselves to the Body of Christ.
The purpose of missionary activity is:
to plant the Word

so that people who have not heard it before
    might believe and be baptized.
We sometimes call this work "evangelization,"
    which means just that:
    to announce God's wonderful Word.
This is different from pastoral work
    among those who already believe
    and from ecumenical work,
        which seeks to bring all Christians
        into a common family.
Pastoral and ecumenical work are necessary though
    in order for missionary work to proceed.
7 We believe that God's plan for human salvation
    is wrapped up in knowing Christ,
    that everyone is called to Christ
    and to the Catholic Church.
Therefore, whoever knows this,
    whoever is called to be in Christ's family
    but refuses to enter the Church,
        cannot find wholeness and eternal life.
All members of the Church are required
    to announce this
    so God's plan can be fulfilled.

8 Missionary activity springs from the very heart
    of what it means to be human,
    to search for the true meaning of life,
    for each person's divine calling.
The Gospel and the Church
    provide access to Christ,
    who supplies what the heart desires most.
9 The time for missionary activity, therefore,
    is now!
For we live in these days

between the first and second appearances
    of Christ.
And the work of the Church
    to preach and celebrate Eucharist
    makes Christ present in this interim.
In this, all of history,
    all cultures and peoples,
    everything on earth
        is made more noble
        and is directed toward that time
        when God will be all in all.

Chapter Two
MISSION WORK ITSELF

10 The Church knows that there remains
    a gigantic missionary goal:
    two billion people on earth
        have still not heard the Word.
Some of these people follow
    one of the world's great religions
    and some have no notion of God at all.
To all of them, the Church wants to be present
    as Christ was present to us.

Article One: Christian Witness

11 The Church is present among these groups
    through its members
    who give witness to Christ
    by their style of life.
Therefore, let them be present by esteem and love,

sharing cultural and social life,
familiar with their traditions.
They should awaken in their sisters and brothers
a sense of awe for the divine
and a yearning for truth and love.
In this way, those present among these people
or sent to them as missionaries
can learn what gifts God has given
to these others
and at the same time
add the light of the Gospel.

12 The presence of Christians
among non-Christians
should be animated by love
just as Christ was lovingly present.
The Church desires to be one with every person,
regardless of race or situation,
especially with the poor and afflicted.
The Church shares their joys and sorrows;
it knows their longings;
it suffers with all.
Therefore, church members should cooperate
in the development of peoples everywhere,
educating children;
working for justice;
ending famine, ignorance, and disease.
It wants to work closely and cooperatively,
without interference,
with governments and agencies,
including non-Christian ones,
in promoting human dignity,
in teaching moral truths,
and in striving for peace.

Article Two: Preaching the Gospel and Assembling God's People

13 When the Holy Spirit opens their hearts,
    and someone gives witness to Christ,
    non-Christians may freely come to believe.
This moment of conversion,
    of coming to believe,
    is only a first step for them on a spiritual journey
    which should be gradual in the catechumenate.
It may involve disruption and, at the same time, joy.

The Church forbids that anyone be forced to join it
    and also forbids the use of sly techniques
    to attract people
        and at the same time also insists
        that anyone who wants to
            must be free to join the Church.
14 Those who do choose freely to come forward
    are to be admitted through the rites
    of the catechumenate.
The catechumenate is not simply a theology course
    but is a formation tool,
    a sort of apprenticeship through which
        people come to know Christ,
        the Christian people,
        and the Christian lifestyle.
Then, slowly, through the rites,
    catechumens are joined to Christ.
We at this council are restoring the catechumenate
    for this very reason,
    so that those coming to Christ
    might properly celebrate the Paschal Mystery
        in the Easter season
        and be reborn in faith.

This is the responsibility of the whole Christian people,
   not just the priests.

Article Three: Forming the Christian Community

15 Missionaries are to establish communities
   of the faithful
   which have the threefold presence of Christ:
      priestly or prayerful presence,
      prophetic or teaching presence,
      and royal or servant presence.
These communities are a sign of God's presence
   and help the Word take deep root.
They should be able to sustain themselves
   and be profoundly incorporated into local culture.
They should also have an ecumenical spirit
   and even assist other Christians
   in expressing a common faith.
They should collaborate with others
   in bringing about a just social order,
   without racial or national prejudice.
Laypeople have a special role to play in this
   since they live in the world.
But it is not enough simply to live peaceably,
   for it is also necessary to announce the Gospel
   in concrete, explicit ways.
Finally, as much as possible,
   vocations from among local people
   are to be fostered and developed.

16 Young men who come forward
   to be priests should be well trained
   for their work.
As much as possible, their training should be local

and should include Scripture,
    an understanding of their culture,
    a spirit of ecumenism,
    church administration,
    and pastoral work.
Where appropriate, the diaconate should be restored.

[17] Likewise, catechists are very important,
    and schools should be established to train them.
They play an indispensable role today
    in the work of the Church,
    and they must have access to ongoing training
    and to just and adequate compensation.

[18] And, finally, religious life should also be fostered
    as the Church is established
    so that the rich treasures it offers
        may be available to all.
The contemplative life may also take root
    in certain places,
    and we support this.

Chapter Three
PARTICULAR CHURCHES

[19] The measure of success in establishing a new community
    is the congregation's stability and firmness.
Stability results from a community
    that has enough resources—
    human and otherwise—
    to meet its own needs, creating a place
        where faith,

Liturgy,
and love are present.
Families in these mature communities
are nurseries of lay ministries
and vocations to the priesthood and religious life.
The bishop and clergy,
along with religious men and women,
are sufficient—though still never adequate—
to meet most local needs.
They link the young Church to the universal Church
and increase the Mystical Body.

Because most young Churches are in places
that are very poor, however,
they continue to need money and personnel
from the rest of the Church
to survive and thrive.

[20] All particular Churches live among others
who are not Christian
and are to be a sign of Christ to them.
The bishop, therefore, should know his flock
and adapt his practice of evangelization
to keep it effective.
Priests likewise should offer themselves for service,
especially to those who need them most,
and they should cooperate with missionaries
from foreign lands.
Religious women and men
and laypeople, too,
should have the same devotion to local needs.
In all cases, bishops should see to it that ministers
are properly trained,
suited to their work,

and in close communication with each other
    and with local groups.
As soon as possible, every young Church
    should send missionaries abroad
    in order to deeply participate
        in the universal mission of Christ.
21 No Church is fully established or mature
    that does not have a working laity,
    for laypeople belong at once to Christ
        as well as to their local culture
        where social progress occurs.
The main duty of Christian laypeople,
    whether men or women,
    is the witness of their everyday life
        lived in their home nations,
        among people they know well,
        and in a culture which is theirs.
In this everyday life, they give witness to Christ
    by being both one with their neighbors
    and at the same time one with the Church.
Laypeople also work in parish ministry
    where they cooperate with their pastors,
    working together to maintain their Church.
22 The beauty of Christian missionary work
    is the gift the universal Church receives
    from the young, emerging Churches.
The local customs and traditions,
    the wisdom and learning of the people,
    the local arts and sciences—
        all this contributes to the wealth
        of the human family
        and to the glory of God.
By paying attention to these gifts,
    the whole Church will grow wiser

and more tolerant
and gain a new perspective.
As a result, avenues will be opened for all people
and local customs will be preserved,
giving local Churches their own place
within the universal Church
without compromising our unity.

Chapter Four
MISSIONARIES

23 All Christians are called to spread the faith,
but some are specially called for this work,
whether as individuals or in groups.
Those called thus are endowed
with the appropriate disposition,
character,
and talent for this work.
24 Those sent to mission lands give up everything
for the sake of the Gospel
and become ambassadors for Christ.
By their words and lifestyle,
they do their work,
forgoing much and sometimes suffering
but always keeping their eye on the goal.
God empowers and strengthens people for this work.

25 Missionaries should be trained for their work,
becoming prayerful,
patient,
strong of heart,
willing to bear solitude,
gladly able to shoulder their duties.

They should have a sympathetic heart
    and an open mind,
    combined with great dedication.
Missionaries should so live the Paschal Mystery,
    should so die in Christ,
    that those they touch may live in Christ!
26 They should know the Scriptures well
    and embrace the doctrine of the Church
    and be well trained for their work.
They should understand diversity,
    yet be deeply rooted in universality,
    be open to varied cultures,
        yet know the oneness we share
        in Christ's Body.
They should understand the place to which they go
    and love its traditions and history,
    esteeming the wisdom, language, and customs
        of the local people.
And, above all, one preparing for this work
    must learn missiology:
    the art of spreading the Gospel effectively,
    both in the classroom and in the field.

27 Missionaries do not work as individuals
    but always out of some kind of community,
    whether organized as an institute
        or as an outgrowth of diocesan generosity.

Chapter Five
PLANNING MISSIONARY ACTIVITY

28 All the Christian people should work as missionaries
    according to their particular talents.

29 The world's bishops are the ones responsible
    to see to it that the Gospel is proclaimed,
    and toward this end,
    there should be one coordinating body:
        The Propagation of the Faith.
This office, working with Eastern Churches,
    should plan and promote missionary work,
        calling forth vocations,
        offering worldwide communications,
        recruiting workers,
        raising money,
        and planning for the needs of the world.
This curia-level office should make use
    of modern means of research in
        theology,
        methodology,
        and pastoral procedure.
It should consult the world's bishops,
    religious superiors,
    and other experts.
Religious women should be consulted in particular,
    in addition to laypeople.
30 Bishops should promote missionary activity
    but should also allow spontaneous zeal
    to be preserved and fostered.
Local bishops should establish pastoral councils
    to guide them.
31 Conferences of bishops should also work together
    to ensure that missionary work is supported.

32 Where a particular institute has committed itself
    to a missionary task,
    the local bishop remains the authority,
        and care should be taken as local clergy

become numerous enough for the work
 to have an orderly transition.
33 In areas where various missionaries are working,
 they should coordinate their efforts
 to save both energy and money.
34 This council wants all missionaries
 to be well trained for their work
 in ethnology,
  linguistics,
  local history,
  sociology,
  and pastoral skills.

Chapter Six
MISSIONARY COOPERATION

35 Because, as we have already said,
 the Church is missionary by its nature
 and because the work of spreading the Gospel
  is so basic to the People of God,
  we call everyone to a deep renewal!
36 The first and most important duty, however,
 is not missionary work,
 but to lead a profoundly Christian life!
By this everyday witness to Christ,
 others will be attracted to the Word
 and a renewal will sweep the Church.
Then the Church will truly become
 the "salt of the earth"
 and the "light of the world."
And this living, everyday witness of the common life
 will be more effective and powerful

if it is in unison with other Christians
and if the modern means of social communication
    are properly employed
      to let current church members hear the voice
      of those who cry, "Help us!"
37 It is also the responsibility of parishes and dioceses,
    however,
    to develop a missionary spirit.
The renewal of the whole Church depends on this:
    that local parishes extend themselves
    in charity and love
    to the ends of the earth
      by sending workers to the harvest
      and supporting them.
This self-giving will give them a new interior life.

38 Here is how this will happen:
    First, as we already said here,
    the bishops have a primary responsibility
    to see that this is done
    because their consecration is not for a single diocese
      but for the good of the whole Church.
The bishop is the leader
    who calls forth volunteers for mission work,
    who generously sends even his best priests,
    and who supports the financial needs they have.
Bishops' conferences should coordinate this,
    finance it,
    and expand it.
39 Second, priests, too, share in the
    priestly or prayerful,
    prophetic or teaching,
    and royal or servant work
      of Christ in the world.

Their very lives, therefore, are consecrated
    to mission work,
    no matter where they live.
They should organize their pastoral activity
    in such a way
    that the Gospel is spread by it,
        stirring up among the faithful
        a zeal for this.
Seminary programs should teach about this
    in their dogmatic,
        biblical,
        moral,
        and historical departments.
40 Third, religious men and women—
    both active and contemplative—
    play a great role in mission work, too,
        for they have had the greatest share
        in spreading the Gospel so far.
Those who are contemplative
    pray for the conversion of souls,
    and those who are active
        can broaden their activity
        and be sure their lifestyle is a witness.
Secular institutes can dedicate themselves
    to evangelization as well.
41 And fourth, laypeople can increase
    their understanding of mission needs,
    work as teachers and social laborers there,
    provide socio-economic development,
    and advance the study of history and science
        to the benefit of mission lands.

Conclusion

42 Through the efforts of those who believe
   may all the world come to know Christ
   and be afire with divine love!

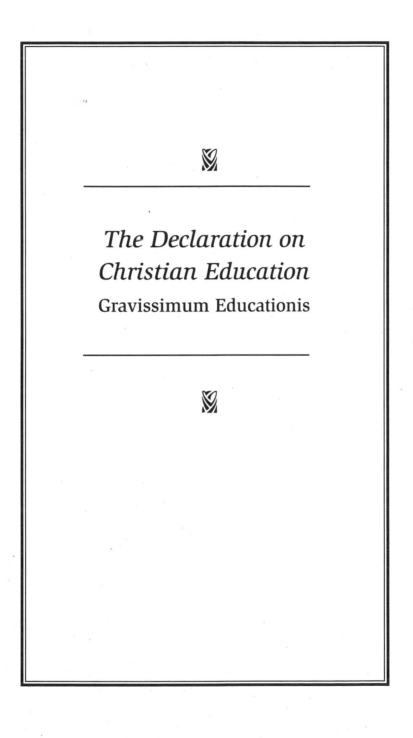

The Declaration on Christian Education
Gravissimum Educationis

Chapter Eleven

※

PART ONE: BACKGROUND

No group of pronouncements from the Church has gone further to claim for its mission the teaching of humankind than the documents of Vatican II. Throughout the documents, the role of Christ the Prophet—that one who speaks for God—has been lifted up and identified as a principal work of the Church. In other words, this might be called the "teaching function" of the Church.

The *Declaration on Christian Education* deals, however, with formal education, especially as it is performed in schools. Aware that a postconciliar commission would lay out the details, this document was designed to give only major principles of Christian education. Therefore, little in the document sounds "new," and its tone is somewhat less pastoral and more technical than other council documents.

For some, the fact that a more forward-looking program was not laid out in the *Declaration on Christian Education* may be disappointing. Such a program might have included, for example, the ecumenical dimensions of Catholic education or the place of the catechumenate and liturgical rites in teaching.

Nonetheless, because of the importance of education in the Church's overall work, this document takes its place among the sixteen promulgated by Pope John XXIII and Pope Paul VI during Vatican II.

The document was introduced for debate on November 17, 1964, during the third session of Vatican II. Because it provided only principles, most council fathers found it generally favorable and made only minor changes to the original texts.

The council eventually approved the document by a vote of 2,290 to 35. The pope promulgated the *Declaration on Christian Education* on October 28, 1965.

PART TWO: PARAPHRASE TEXT

*F*rom the Vatican II document
promulgated on October 28, 1965

Introduction

1 Education is important to people
   all around the world.
It is basic to human progress
   and social development,
   and the means of education
   are changing and improving rapidly.
There are still many people in the world
   who do not have adequate access to education
   even though they want it,
      both adults and young people.
Nonetheless, the right to education
   is frequently being proclaimed,
   schools are increasing in number,

new methods of education are emerging,
and attempts are being made to extend
    the benefit of education to all.
We now offer some principles,
    which will have to be elaborated later,
    to guide Christian education.

Declaration

First, every person regardless of age,
    race,
    or social conditions
        has an inalienable right
        to an education.
This education should be appropriate
    for each person's proper destiny
    and suited to each one's talents,
        gender,
        cultural background,
        and ancestral heritage.
Such an education will inevitably lead
    to greater human harmony and peace
    as people come to understand one another.
It is a special concern of ours
    that young people be assisted
    in the full development of their persons:
        physical,
        moral,
        sexual,
        social,
        and intellectual.
We affirm that children and young people

have a right to weigh moral values
in their own consciences
    and to embrace them
    by personal choice
    as they come to know and love God
       more fully.
2 Second, all the faithful likewise have a right
    to a Christian education,
    advancing in understanding the faith
    and growing mature as faithful persons.
We especially affirm liturgical worship
    as a means toward this end.
Pastors have a serious duty to be certain
    that all who are in their care
    are offered a Christian education,
       especially young people.
3 Third, parents who give life to children
    have a firm duty
    to educate them as well.
Parents are, in fact, the first and foremost educators
    of their children
    within a family atmosphere
      animated with love,
       providing a well-rounded formation.
The family can be called the first school
    of those social virtues
    that every society needs.
The Christian family is enriched by the grace
    of the sacrament of matrimony
    and is the place where children are first taught
      to know and love God
      and to know and love their neighbor.
Here they come to understand human companionship,
    here they are introduced into civic life,

and here they are initiated into the parish community.
And while the family is basic,
    it also needs the support and help
    of the wider community and society
        which oversees the work of parents
        and provides assistance to them.
And while the family and society have these roles,
    the Church, too, has a role
    in helping provide the kind of education
        through which all know Christ
        and develop their full humanness.

4 We will now comment more broadly
    on the Church's role.

For the Church, catechetical training
    is the foremost educational concern,
    giving clarity and vigor to the faith.
We seek to make use of the means for education
    already present in the human community,
    such as the media,
        social groups devoted to human growth,
        and especially schools.
5 The school is key because it
    provides intellectual development,
    ripens the ability for moral judgments,
    teaches about history and culture,
    and prepares people for professions.
It also allows students to mingle with others
    of diverse backgrounds
    and becomes a center for community life.
Teaching is, therefore, a great vocation!

6 Parents should have true freedom

in selecting schools.
Public authority should provide that everyone
    has access to a school
    and should provide qualified teachers
    and should avoid "school monopolies,"
        providing choices instead.
The faithful play a role in governing this
    by their active participation
    in community and school affairs.

7 We have a special solicitude for children
    being trained in settings
    that are not explicitly organized
    according to their religious tradition.
In some cases, this refers to non-Catholic students
    in Catholic schools
    and in others, it refers to Catholic students
        in non-Catholic schools.
Whatever the case, parents retain the right
    to educate their children
    according to the moral and religious faith
        of each family.

8 The Church claims the right to conduct schools
    of every type and level
    and has the same aim in doing so
    that the society has:
        the development of youth.
But the Church has other aims as well:
    to provide an atmosphere animated by the Gospel
        in which one might express faith,
        grow as a human,
        and order his or her life
            according to the plan of God.

This council also recalls, however,
    that in operating schools,
    the Church also must ensure freedom of conscience,
        the protection of parental rights,
        and the progress of culture itself.
Teachers play a very important role
    as partners with parents
    in providing both training and friendship
        as children grow and mature.
Catholic parents should entrust their children
    to Catholic schools when possible.

9 While we certainly support primary and secondary schools,
    we also see the need for other kinds of schools,
    especially technical and catechetical ones,
    as well as for those with special needs,
        and we urge their development as well.
We also offer a cordial and affectionate hand
    to non-Catholic students in our schools.
10 We also support colleges and universities
    where research in human development occurs
    and where faith and science swim together.
New social and scientific questions should be pursued,
    and all of society helped by them.
A department of theology should exist
    in every Catholic college or university,
    and such schools should exist all over the world.
Student centers for pastoral ministries
    should be established at all such schools
    whether or not they are Catholic.
11 We look to those who are studying theology
    not only to prepare students for priesthood
    but also to advance our understanding
        and deepen our faith.

Hence, a more profound understanding
of sacred revelation is possible
and dialogue will be fostered
among all Christians.
Faculties in the sacred sciences should, therefore,
update their methods and teaching style
and open the way for searching inquiries.
12 We also call for more coordination among schools,
whether Catholic or not,
to advance knowledge and understanding.

Conclusion

We call on young people everywhere
to consider becoming teachers
and to devote themselves generously
to this great human need.
And we also thank those priests,
religious women and men,
and laypeople
who have been so devoted
for so many years.
Carry on, we say, this tradition!

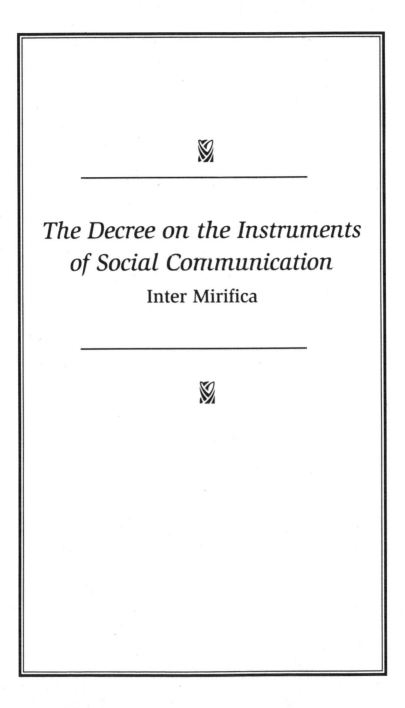

The Decree on the Instruments of Social Communication

Inter Mirifica

Chapter Twelve

Part One: Background

*W*ithin the lifetimes of many who are still living, the main avenues of social communication were local, rather than global as they are today. Whenever the Church has addressed social communications or social groupings in the past, it has concerned itself with groups such as the family, the neighborhood, the parish, or even the nation—but not with groups emerging from global technology.

One could argue that today there are social groups that are identified by their devotion to a particular television program, and in fact, such devotees of certain programs (such as *Star Trek*) do form a social group together.

There are also groups emerging today who have been socialized by their participation in certain computer-based, "internet" programs. This new level of socialization transcends family, neighborhood, ethnic group, or nation. The *Decree on the Instruments of Social Communication* addresses this new phenomenon of modern life.

The flat tone of the document, however, does not possess the richness of later council pronouncements, such as the documents on religious liberty or the one on the Church in the modern world. Perhaps this document is simply a "first step" in the Church's desire to understand and offer guidance in the use of modern means of communication.

The council passed the document with a vote of 1,960 to 164, and the pope promulgated it on December 4, 1963. It was one of the first two documents the council issued.

The negative vote was the largest for any document. Why? Perhaps because the council fathers did not consider the matter central in their proceedings and perhaps because they may have desired to move the *Decree on the Instruments of Social Communication* off the agenda, with or without more agreement.

PART TWO: PARAPHRASE TEXT

*F*rom the Vatican II document
promulgated on December 4, 1963

1 In these modern times,
    human genius has produced
    an astonishing array of technological inventions!
Some of these have real impact on people
    because they open up new and powerfully effective
    avenues of communication
        by which all kinds of ideas,
            information,
            and mandates
                are communicated.
The Church welcomes this!
    It also watches it with concern.
The ones we watch most are those
    that can reach the largest audiences
    (indeed, some can reach the whole of humanity!)

such as the press,
     movies,
     radio,
     television,
     and similar media.
These are the means of social communication.

2 In order to assist the human family as a whole
     in coming to terms with this new technology,
     this council now turns its attention
          to these instruments of communication.
We realize how much they can benefit humankind
     but also how much harm they can do
          if used wrongly.
Therefore, we will propose certain directives
     and principles for their proper use.

Chapter One
ON THE TEACHING OF THE CHURCH

3 Because the Catholic Church
     has the task of preaching the Gospel
     to the whole world,
          it claims the right to have and use
          all instruments of social communication
          and to guide humankind in their use.
It is the responsibility of the Church's pastors
     to assist the culture in using these instruments
     in such a way that they benefit people.
And it is the layperson's duty
     to use them as a means
          of animating the world with a Christian spirit.

4 Those who employ the media
must be thoroughly aware of the ethics involved.
They should consider the subject matter
alongside the means with which it is communicated
and be certain they have a good intention,
know their audience,
understand the place in which it is received,
and use proper timing to deliver the message.
They should also be aware of the powerful
and sometimes unconscious influence
their message will have on people.
This will allow the users to perceive what is really being said,
judge it properly,
and reject it, if necessary.

5 There are three primary areas of our concern:

First, there is a special need to deliver the "news"
accurately and completely
to allow people to understand their times
and contribute to the common good.
In fact, people have a right to information
about public affairs that affect them,
but such news should be given in such a way
that human dignity is not compromised
and it is delivered with charity.
6 Second, art should be judged according to morality
and give absolute allegiance to it
since the moral order touches humans
in their totality
and can lead humans to a rich life.
7 Third, when communicating moral evils,
restraint should be employed
to avoid doing harm rather than good.
8 Because of the influence of public opinion today,

every citizen must do
what justice and charity requires in this matter.

9 Consumers of the media
    must choose what is good
    and reject what is not
    to avoid rewarding those using the media
        to do harm.
10 Consumers should be moderate in their use
    of the media
    and should assist the young to make proper choices.
The goal should be to be ever more conscious
    of what they see, hear, and read.
11 The main moral duty, however,
    on the development of ethical media
    rests with those who produce it.
They have an important leadership role
    in the human race
    and should take care to be certain that what they do
        contributes to the common good.
They should be careful to have competent people
    in charge of religious programming.

12 Civil authority, too, has a role here.
They should, first and foremost,
    protect the public's right to information
    through assuring freedom of the press.
They should foster religion,
    the humanities,
    and the free exercise of lawful rights.
And they should protect society against the harm
    that can result from misuse of media
    by enacting and enforcing laws to this effect.
Young people, in particular, should be protected.

Chapter Two
ON THE PASTORAL ACTIVITY OF THE CHURCH

13 The Church itself should also use the media effectively,
    especially pastors in preaching the Word,
    and laypeople by contributing their expertise.
14 A faithful Catholic press should be developed
    with the clear goal in mind
        of forming,
        strengthening,
        and spreading public views
        that are in harmony with the Church.
Films that provide relaxation,
    as well as culture and art,
    should be encouraged.
Decent radio and television programming
    should likewise be fostered,
    including Catholic stations when possible.
Theater productions should serve
    the cultural and moral development
    of their audiences.
15 Toward this end,
    laypeople should be schooled
    in art, doctrine, and ethics;
        actors trained to enrich human culture;
        and critics taught
        to take moral issues into account
        when passing judgments.
16 Schools should train young people,
    seminaries their students,
    and lay groups their members
        in the proper use of the media.
17 Catholics are bound to provide financial support
    to the development of Catholic media outlets

and to provide technical support as they can.

18 Every diocese in the world
   is to have one day each year
   on which it offers training on these matters
   and asks for contributions to support the work.

19 The pope has a special office to oversee this.

20 Bishops have the duty of overseeing the media
   in their own dioceses as well.

21 The council directs that every nation have an office
   to oversee the general needs of that country,
   under the management of the bishops
   but employing laypeople skilled in this field.

22 Various national groups should join together
   on international levels when appropriate.

Conclusion

23 An instruction from the Vatican office
   pertaining to this matter
   is to be prepared.

24 We trust, furthermore, that all people
   will welcome and observe these principles.
We urge all involved with the media
   to use them only for good
   because the fate of humanity
      rests more and more on their influence.
In all this, then,
   may Christ be glorified!

Appendix One

※

A Brief Summary of the Documents of Vatican II

PART ONE: THE FOUR CONSTITUTIONS

These major documents set direction for the whole Church.

1. Dogmatic Constitution on the CHURCH

(In Latin, *Lumen Gentium*.)

Approved on November 21, 1964, by a vote of 2,151 to 5.

This strong document was argued by the council from the first day to its passage. It was widely supported in the end and set a major new focus for the Church. It treated several key aspects of the Catholic theology of Church.

(1) The Church, this document says, is a mystery, i.e., "a reality imbued with the hidden presence of God." It is a sacrament: a visible, tangible, audible sign of the invisible, intangible, inaudible divinity. (2) The Church, furthermore, is the whole People of God, including but not identical with its hierarchy alone. (3) Bishops, for their part, are to act collegially, together with the pope, the bishop of Rome. (4) By their very vocation, the laity seek the Reign of God by engaging in "temporal" affairs and ordering them according to the plan of God. (5) The call to holiness is a call to

everyone. (6) The consecrated life of women and men religious is a particular gift to the Church. (7) Christians share the Church with those who have died and who now share life with God in heaven. (8) The memory of Mary is to hold a place of reverence for all.

The document contains 69 articles
in the following eight chapters:

a. The Mystery of the Church
b. On the People of God
c. On the Hierarchical Structure of the Church and in Particular, on the Episcopate
d. The Laity
e. The Universal Call to Holiness in the Church
f. Religious
g. The Eschatological Nature of the Pilgrim Church and Its Union with the Church in Heaven
h. The Blessed Virgin Mary, Mother of God, in the Mystery of Christ and the Church

2. Dogmatic Constitution on DIVINE REVELATION

(In Latin, *Dei Verbum.*)

Approved on November 18, 1965, by a vote of 2,344 to 6.

This strong document states that the Church moves forward in time, developing an ever deeper understanding of what is handed down about the Reign of God and always finding new ways of expressing that.

The document emphasizes that the Word of God is the foundation of divine revelation, and it corrects the understanding that there are two equal sources of revelation, namely, tradition and Scripture. It clarifies that the Word of God is found both in sacred tradition as well as in sacred Scripture. God speaks to us, this document explains, in word and deed and calls forth a response from us. We call this response "faith" and through faith we entrust our whole selves to God. This faith is handed on to all generations by *living* traditions. This faith is contained in one sacred deposit, expressed through the teaching office of the Church whose role and duty it is to serve the Word of God.

The document contains 26 articles in the following six chapters:

a. Revelation Itself
b. Handing On Divine Revelation
c. Sacred Scripture: Its Inspiration and Divine Interpretation
d. The Old Testament
e. The New Testament
f. Sacred Scripture in the Life of the Church

3. Constitution on the SACRED LITURGY

(In Latin, *Sacrosanctum Concilium*.)

Approved on December 4, 1963, by a vote of 2,147 to 4.

This constitution has had the most influence in the emergence of the laity after the council because it updates the Mass, including the role of the laity as ministers in the Liturgy, thus bringing about a sea change in Catholic lay self-identity.

The document seeks (1) to give vigor to the Christian life of the faithful, (2) to adapt what is changeable to the needs of today, (3) to promote union among all who believe in Christ, and (4) to strengthen the Church's mission to all humankind. The constitution declares that the Mass (the Liturgy) is the source and summit of the Christian life.

Therefore, for the Liturgy to be effective, the faithful must (1) be well disposed, (2) know what they are doing, and (3) participate. The document established that some things are changeable (language, books, prayers, music, persons, and places) while some are not (Scripture, bread, wine, prayer over the gifts, eucharistic prayer, communion). It also establishes vernacular in worship. The laity cannot participate in Latin. The document restores the Eucharist as an *act* rather than as a *static devotional object*. This means a downplaying of devotions outside of Mass: rosary, benediction, and so on. The lessening of these devotions is felt very strongly by the average Catholic.

Several "instructions" on implementing the document follow it. The first of these instructions was published before the end of the council.

The document contains 130 articles
in the following eight chapters:

a. General Principles for Restoration and
   Promotion of the Sacred Liturgy
b. The Most Sacred Mystery of the Eucharist
c. Other Sacraments and the Sacramentals
d. The Divine Office
e. The Liturgical Year
f. Sacred Music
g. Sacred Art and Furnishings
h. Appendix: A Declaration of the Second Vatican
   Council on the Revision of the Calendar

4. Pastoral Constitution on the
CHURCH IN THE MODERN WORLD

(In Latin, *Gaudium et Spes*.)

Approved on December 7, 1965, by a vote of 2,309 to 75.

This important historic document speaks to the Church and to all people about the hopes and dreams of the human family. It is the first document issued by such a council to address the whole world.

"The joy and hope, the grief and anxiety of the people of this age, especially those who are poor or in any way afflicted, this is the joy and hope, the grief and anxiety of the followers of Christ." Modern Christians must look at and trust the signs of the times and understand the world in which they live. (Contrast this with Pius IX's *Syllabus of Errors* in 1864, which says that the pope "cannot and should not be reconciled and come to terms with progress, liberalism, and modern civilization.")

The human person is dignified but many still suffer. Human "conscience is the most secret core and sanctuary of a person where he or she is alone with God." But there is a mysterious aspect to human nature, and conscience is not easily discerned. Modern people live together in a global community of persons for which there must be made available everything necessary for leading a truly human life. Every type of discrimination is to be overcome and eradicated as contrary to God's intent. Science does not conflict with faith.

The Church lives and acts in the world. "Let there be no false opposition between professional and social activities on the one part, and religious life on the other." It is not "the world against the Church." It is "the world together with the Church."

The document contains 93 articles
in the following nine chapters:

a. The Dignity of the Human Person
b. The Community of Humankind
c. Humans' Activity throughout the World
d. The Role of the Church in the Modern World
e. Fostering the Nobility of Marriage and the
   Family
f. The Proper Development of Culture
g. Economic and Social Life
h. The Life of the Political Community
i. The Fostering of Peace and the Promotion of a
   Community of Nations

PART TWO: THE NINE DECREES

These are significant documents, to be used in further
reflection. They set a pace and direction for further discussion.

1. Decree on the Instruments of
SOCIAL COMMUNICATION

(In Latin, *Inter Mirifica.*)

Approved on December 4, 1963, by a vote of 1,960 to 164.

This relatively weak document is condescending in tone and
is addressed to the media and those who control it. The
document calls for the Church to use modern media to
preach the Gospel. It also calls for the faithful to reject what

is ungodly in the media. The document is seen by most theologians as out of touch with the overall theology of the council. It was one of the first to be passed.

The document contains 24 articles
in the following two chapters:

a. On the Teaching of the Church
b. On the Pastoral Activity of the Church

2. Decree on ECUMENISM

(In Latin, *Unitatis Redintegratio*.)

Approved on November 21, 1964, by a vote of 2,137 to 11.

This document represents a major move forward for the Church. It seeks restoration of ties with other Christians rather than their return to Rome. The document admits that blame for separation exists on both sides and calls for a change of heart to make ecumenism possible. Eucharistic sharing may at times be necessary for the gaining of the grace of unity (n. 8). The document encourages dialogue and calls for the Roman Church to reform itself as part of the process of reunion.

The document contains 24 articles
in the following three chapters:

a. Catholic Principles on Ecumenism
b. The Practice of Ecumenism
c. Churches and Ecclesial Communities Separated from the Roman Apostolic See

3. Decree on the EASTERN CATHOLIC CHURCHES

(In Latin, *Orientalium Ecclesiarum.*)

Approved on November 21, 1964, by a vote of 2,110 to 39.

This minor document gives Rome's perspective on the six main Eastern Rite Churches: Chaldean, Syrian, Maronite, Coptic, Armenian, and Byzantine. It states an ardent desire for reconciliation and clearly proclaims the equality of the Eastern and Western traditions.

The document contains 30 articles
in the following six chapters:

a. The Individual Churches or Rites
b. Preservation of the Spiritual Heritage of the Eastern Churches
c. Eastern Rite Patriarchs
d. The Disciplines of the Sacraments
e. Divine Worship
f. Relations with the Brethren of the Separated Churches

4. Decree on the BISHOPS' PASTORAL OFFICE in the Church

(In Latin, *Christus Dominus.*)

Approved on October 28, 1965, by a vote of 2,319 to 2.

This is a follow-up document to the one on the Church. It gives a job description for bishops and stresses the need for shared decision making (collegiality). The document also calls for bishops to be servant leaders and establishes diocesan pastoral councils.

The document contains 44 articles
in the following four chapters:

a. The Relationship of Bishops to the Universal
Church
b. Bishops and Their Particular Churches or
Dioceses
c. Concerning Bishops Cooperating for the
Common Good of Many Churches
d. General Directive

5. Decree on PRIESTLY FORMATION

(In Latin, *Optatam Totius.*)

Approved on October 28, 1965, by a vote of 2,318 to 3.

This document revises the rules for seminary training which
had been established at the Council of Trent 450 years
earlier. It calls for training in Scripture, pastoral counseling,
ecumenism, history, and personal formation. The document
also allows for local training guidelines to produce priests
more ready to deal with local pastoral realities.

The document contains 22 articles
in the following seven chapters:

a. The Program of Priestly Training to Be
Undertaken by Each Country
b. The Urgent Fostering of Priestly Vocations
c. The Setting Up of Major Seminaries
d. The Careful Development of the Spiritual
Training
e. The Revision of Ecclesiastical Studies

f. The Promotion of Strictly Pastoral Training
g. Training to Be Achieved after the Course of
    Studies

6. Decree on the APPROPRIATE RENEWAL OF RELIGIOUS LIFE

(In Latin, *Perfectae Caritatis.*)

Approved on October 28, 1965, by a vote of 2,321 to 4.

This document urges religious women and men (1) to return to their roots, that is, their reasons for being founded and (2) to adjust to the needs of changing times in the modern Church. It does not repeat the teaching of Trent that religious life is a superior state to that of the married.

The document contains 25 articles all in one chapter.

7. Decree on the APOSTOLATE OF THE LAITY

(In Latin, *Apostolicam Actuositatem.*)

Approved on November 18, 1965, by a vote of 2,305 to 2.

Although this document has less influence than the constitutions, it is important as the first document in the history of ecumenical councils to address itself to anyone other than the Church's own clergy. The document declares that by virtue of their baptisms, the laity have a ministry, not merely a sharing in the ministry of the ordained. This lengthy document details how the apostolic work of the laity is to proceed and how laypersons are to be prepared for this work.

It also places great emphasis on the importance of each person's role in the establishment of the Reign of God.

The document contains 33 articles
in the following seven chapters:

a. The Vocation of the Laity to the Apostolate
b. Objectives
c. The Various Fields of the Apostolate
d. The Various Forms of the Apostolate
e. External Relationships
f. Formation for the Apostolate
g. Exhortation

8. Decree on the MINISTRY AND LIFE OF PRIESTS

(In Latin, *Presbyterorum Ordinis.*)

Approved on December 7, 1965, by a vote of 2,390 to 4.

This last-minute document does not address the social needs of today's priests. (A later synod in 1970 tried to make up for this weakness.) It calls on priests to support the laity and reaffirms celibacy for priests of the Latin Rite. The document says that, although it is not demanded by the very nature of the priesthood, celibacy seems "suitable."

The document contains 22 articles
in the following four chapters:

a. The Priesthood in the Mission of the Church
b. The Ministry of Priests
c. The Life of Priests
d. Conclusion and Exhortation

9. Decree on the Church's MISSIONARY ACTIVITY

(In Latin, *Ad Gentes.*)

Approved on December 7, 1965, by a vote of 2,394 to 5.

This document encourages retaining local religious customs and incorporating the Gospel into them, a radical idea. It also states that the whole Church is missionary, meaning that all the People of God are called to introduce others to the faith. The document tries to consolidate all the strains of ecclesiology discussed elsewhere.

The document contains 41 articles
in the following six chapters:
   a.   Doctrinal Principles
   b.   Mission Work Itself
   c.   Particular Churches
   d.   Missionaries
   e.   Planning Missionary Activity
   f.   Cooperation

PART THREE: THE THREE DECLARATIONS

These statements of theological position are important for their influence on future dialogue.

1. Declaration on CHRISTIAN EDUCATION

(In Latin, *Gravissimum Educationis.*)

Approved on October 28, 1965, by a vote of 2,290 to 35.

This weak document leaves most of the work to postconciliar development. It is still under study today.

The document contains 12 articles on these topics:

a. The Meaning of the Universal Right to an Education
b. Christian Education
c. The Authors of Education
d. Various Aids to Christian Education
e. The Importance of Schools
f. The Duties and Rights of Parents
g. Moral and Religious Education in All Schools
h. Catholic Schools
i. Different Types of Catholic Schools
j. Catholic Colleges and Universities
k. Coordination to Be Fostered in Scholastic Matters

2. Declaration on the RELATIONSHIP OF THE CHURCH TO NON-CHRISTIANS

(In Latin, *Nostra Aetate*.)

Approved on October 28, 1965, by a vote of 2,221 to 88.

This earthshaking document began as a statement only about the Church's relations with the Jews but was widened to say that the "truth" is present outside the Body of Christ and is to be respected wherever it is found, mentioning in particular Hinduism, Buddhism, and Islam, as well as Judaism. The Catholic Church, it states, encourages dialogue and opens itself to the contributions of these others. Most importantly, the document states that God loves the Jews and that they cannot be blamed as a race for the death of Jesus. The document condemns every form of persecution or discrimination against the Jews.

The document contains five articles all in one chapter.

3. Declaration on RELIGIOUS FREEDOM

(In Latin, *Dignitatis Humanae*.)

Approved on December 7, 1965, by a vote of 2,308 to 70.

This most controversial of council documents began as a chapter in the document on ecumenism. The document allows for the development of doctrine and says that the freedom of persons requires that no one ever be forced to join the Church. The Church claims freedom for itself in this document, but also for all religious practice of every kind everywhere.

The document contains 15 articles all in one chapter.

Appendix Two

⌘

A Carefully Annotated Reading List
on Vatican II

PART ONE: THE DOCUMENTS

The Documents of Vatican II
Walter M. Abbott, S.J.

Most of the standard writings on the council will use this translation. (Costello Publishing Company, 1975, 1984.)

Vatican Council II
Austin Flannery, O.P.

This is good for postconciliar documents and statements. Also, a second volume shows how the council's decisions are being implemented. (Scholarly Resources, 1975; William B. Eerdmans, New Revised Edition, 1988.)

Decrees of the Ecumenical Councils (two volumes)
ed. Norman P. Tanner, S.J.

This reference book provides English translations of all the documents of each ecumenical council in the entire history of the Church. It has excellent indices. (Sheed & Ward, 1990; Georgetown University Press, 1990.)

Part Two: General Works on the Council

Destination: Vatican II
Thomas More

This highly interactive and detailed CD-ROM includes all major works on Vatican II including Walter Abbott's edition of the documents, the Daybooks, Xavier Rynne, Bill Huebsch's paraphrase text, timelines, biographies, interviews, and much more! (Thomas More Publishing, 1996.)

The Faithful Revolution: Vatican II
Thomas More

This five part video documentary was derived from more than 170 hours of live interviews with many of the council's participants and observers. It tells the story of Vatican II's legacy in an unbiased and complete fashion. (Thomas More Publishing, 1996.)

The Second Vatican Council and the New Catholicism
G. Berkouwer

Berkouwer was an observer at the council, and he has some interesting observations from a non-Catholic point of view. (William B. Eerdmans, 1965.)

The Theology of Vatican II
Dom Christopher Butler

The excellent introduction to this book gives very helpful background for both Vatican I and Vatican II. The work itself is also excellent, but not for beginners. (Darton, Longman & Todd, 1967; Christian Classics, 1981.)

The Joannine Council
Bernard Häring

Häring was one of the liberal *periti* at Vatican II. He pioneered a whole new approach to moral theology. (Herder and Herder, 1963.)

The Council Reform and Reunion
Hans Küng

This work made Küng a household name. He presents the problems and expectations for the council on the eve of Vatican II. The sale of this book in Rome was banned during the first session of the council. (Sheed & Ward, 1961.)

Vatican Council II
Xavier Rynne

This is a detailed account of the proceedings of the council itself and is still the best for accuracy, style, and astute observation. This version is a condensed edition of Rynne's four volumes, one for each session. (Farrar, Straus and Giroux, 1968.)

A Spirituality of Wholeness: The New Look at Grace
Bill Huebsch

This book offers a treatment of the theology of grace which formed the basis of the work done at the council. It is written in easy-to-read sense lines and common English. (Twenty-Third Publications, 1994.)

Rethinking Sacraments: Holy Moments in Daily Living
Bill Huebsch

Another book by the same author in the same style, this volume details the shift in focus which the council enacted in its reform of the traditional seven sacraments of the Church. (Twenty-Third Publications, 1993.)

American Participation in the Second Vatican Council
Vincent Yzermans

This book is a very complete compilation of speeches and other contributions made by U.S. prelates and *periti* during Vatican II. Its index is outstanding. (Sheed & Ward, 1967.)

Vatican II: An Interfaith Appraisal
Edited by John Miller

Miller edited an excellent group of articles, including many that tell the story of the actual debates at the council. To really gain an insight into how the reforms unfolded, read this. The book is out of print but available in used book stores. (Universary of Notre Dame Press and Association Press, 1966.)

A Man Called John
Alden Hatch

No study of the council is complete without reading a biography of John XXIII. This one is brief, readable, and objective. (Hawthorne Books, 1963.)

A Concise History of the Catholic Church

Thomas Bokenkotter

This classic should be on everyone's bookshelf. There is simply no better, more objective postconciliar history of the Church for readability and indexing. (Doubleday, 1977.)

The Church Emerging from Vatican II

Dennis M. Doyle

This is a very well written and easy-to-read treatment of how the council affected the day-to-day life of the Church. Doyle is a scholar on the council and his book makes wide use of anecdotes and stories as a way of situating the council in today's Church. (Twenty-Third Publications, 1994.)

Council Daybook (three volumes)

Edited by Floyd Anderson

For the most complete story of the council's proceedings from the opening speeches to the closing bell, read this. It can be easily browsed and has a very detailed index if one is looking for something specific. It is only available in used book stores. (National Council Welfare Conference, [1962–63] 1965, [1964] 1965, [1965] 1966.)

Council Speeches of Vatican II

Yves Congar, Hans Küng, and Daniel O'Hanlon

Selected by three leading periti, these speeches are also included in the daybooks. But this small volume is more available and easier to hold than they are. (Sheed & Ward, 1964.)

Catholicism
Richard McBrien

It goes without saying that this is a handbook for every Catholic, and it presents the outcomes of Vatican II very faithfully. Everyone should own this book. To make it more affordable, McBrien's book is available in softcover editions. (Winston Press, 1981.)

The Catechism of the Catholic Church

This official, comprehensive treatment of the Catholic faith includes an excellent index which gives generous attention to the impact that Vatican II has had on the modern Church. (Harper San Francisco, 1994.)

Index

Book Two: The Four Constitutions

Book Three: The Decrees and Declarations

Topic	Document	Article
Liturgy		
• the fount and apex of the whole Christian life	Church	11
• its role in Christian growth	Education	2
• presence of Christ in the Church through Liturgy	Liturgy	7
• full, active, knowledgeable participation of laity	Liturgy	11
• a sacrament of unity, not a private function	Liturgy	26
• establishment of local commissions on Liturgy	Liturgy	45
• linking sacred music to liturgical actions	Liturgy	112
• active singing of the people	Liturgy	113
• liturgical year	Liturgy	102, 106, 107
• unity with the communion of saints	Church	50
• as a sign of unity	Liturgy	2
• priestly actions of Christ exercised	Liturgy	7
• connection to preaching	Liturgy	9
• whole Christian life	Liturgy	10
• various functions within the Liturgy	Liturgy	32
• signs chosen by Christ	Liturgy	33
• indigenization of rites	Liturgy	37

TOPIC	DOCUMENT	ARTICLE
• earthly versus heavenly Liturgy	Liturgy	8
• place and function of sermon	Liturgy	35
• adaptation of liturgical rites	Liturgy	23
• music	Liturgy	112
• connection to community life	Religious Life	15
• the teaching of Liturgy	Liturgy	16
• sacramentals	Liturgy	61
• Liturgy of the Word	Liturgy	56
• permission to change and adapt	Liturgy	21–23
• use of local languages (vernacular)	Liturgy	36
• primary role of bishops in providing Eucharist	Bishops	15
also:	Life and Ministry of Priests	5

ECUMENISM

• bishops' role in fostering	Bishops	16
• priests' role in including	Life and Ministry of Priests	9
• ecumenical activity	Missionary Activity	15
• renewal needed with the Church first	Ecumenism	4
• no place for "imprudent zeal"	Ecumenism	24
• call to participate in ecumenical activity	Ecumenism	4
• joining in prayer with others	Ecumenism	8
• understanding theology of others	Ecumenism	9
• great movement toward ecumenism	Ecumenism	1
• defined	Ecumenism	4
• need for new members to nourish openness	Missionary Activity	15
• need for education and theology	Ecumenism	10

LAITY

• laypeople working for the Church	Laity	22

TOPIC	DOCUMENT	ARTICLE
• place of laypeople in their cultures	Laity	29
• Church not able to function without laypeople	Laity	1
• role to play in life and activity of Church	Laity	10
• ordinary lay life as holy	Church	34
• secular duties belong to laypeople	Modern World	43
• apostolate of laypeople	Laity	esp. 1–2, 6, 13–14, 20, 23–25
also:	Communications	18
	Church	13, 35
	Bishops	17, 30
	Missionary Activity	19, 21
	Priestly Formation	6, 20
• contribution of laypeople to life of whole Church	Church	30
• need for laypeople to express opinions	Church	37
• management of temporal affairs of Church	Life and Ministry of Priests	17
• role in evangelization	Laity	31, 33
• establishment of pastoral councils	Bishops	37
• role of priests toward laity	Life and Ministry of Priests	9
also:	Church	30, 33
• harmony of secular and Church life for laity	Church	36
also:	Laity	7–8, 13, 16, 29
	Missionary Activity	21
• role on liturgical commissions	Liturgy	44
• obedience of laity toward hierarchy	Church	37
• responsibilities of laypeople	Laity	1, 6, 17
also:	Church	37, 43
	Modern World	43
	Life and Ministry of Priests	9
	Missionary Activity	15, 21

Topic	Document	Article
	Bishops	10
	Liturgy	100
• active participation in Liturgy	Liturgy	19, 33, 48, 55, 106

ACCULTURATION

• need to express belief in terminology of various peoples	Modern World	44
• need to apply teachings of this council locally	Modern World	91
• call of bishop to become familiar with local situation	Bishops	16
• place for both Eastern and Western traditions	Liturgy	24
• adaptation of Liturgy to local cultures permitted	Liturgy	38, 65

INTERRELIGIOUS DIALOGUE

• those not yet in the Gospel relate to Church	Church	16
• role of bishop in caring for non-Christians	Bishops	16
• brotherly spirit of love for all	Missionary Activity	41
• dialogue with the Jews	Non-Christians	4
• dialogue between Church and non-Christians	Missionary Activity	11, 34, 41
• dialogue between Church and nonbelievers	Modern World	21
• the Church rejects nothing true in other religions	Non-Christians	2

RELIGIOUS FREEDOM

• society must allow religious freedom for all	Church	36
• educational systems must allow freedom	Education	7
• the right to needs and freedoms	Modern World	26

TOPIC	DOCUMENT	ARTICLE
• freedom of religion is for all	Modern World	73, 76
• definition of religious freedom	Religious Liberty	2
• role of government in assuring freedom	Religious Liberty	6
• false religious freedom abuses people	Religious Liberty	7
• roots in revelation of freedom	Religious Liberty	9
• no one is to be forced to join the Church	Missionary Activity	13
• the Church's own freedoms insured	Modern World	42
also:	Bishops	20
	Religious Liberty	13

RENEWAL OF RELIGIOUS LIFE

• men and women religious should be properly trained	Religious Life	18
• renewal of religious life rooted in founders	Religious Life	1–2
• sisters should be equal	Religious Life	15
• vocations should be encouraged	Religious Life	24
• religious and laity harmonize ministry	Laity	23
• testimony of religious to world	Church	31, 46
also:	Religious Life	12, 24
• role of communities in larger Church	Bishops	33
• cooperation with local bishops essential	Bishops	35
• place of chastity in religious life	Religious Life	12
• formation of religious	Religious Life	18
• place of obedience in religious life	Religious Life	14
also:	Bishops	35
• place of poverty in religious life	Religious Life	13

TOPIC	DOCUMENT	ARTICLE
• change of religious habit or garb	Religious Life	17
• spirit of religious life	Religious Life	6–8

PEACE AND JUSTICE

(PEACE . . .)

• role of laity in becoming peacemaker	Church	38
• peace is more than the absence of war	Modern World	78
• peace is based on justice	Modern World	77
• role of military personnel in promoting peace	Modern World	79
• deterrence as a means of promoting peace	Modern World	81
• cooperation of Catholics with others	Modern World	90
• role of bishops in teaching about peace	Bishops	12
• outcome of proper missionary activity	Missionary Activity	8, 12
• need for ecumenism to focus on peacemaking	Ecumenism	12
• norms for establishing peace	Modern World	77–90
• role of education in leading to peace	Education	1

(JUSTICE . . .)

• as a virtue for all laypeople	Laity	4, 8, 14
also:	Church	9, 36
• social order must be based on justice	Modern World	26, 35, 38–39, 63
• governments' role in promoting justice	Religious Liberty	6–7
• priests' obligation to practice justice	Life and Ministry of Priests	12
• justice as a revealed truth	Revelation	11

TOPIC	DOCUMENT	ARTICLE
• the Church's role in promoting justice	Modern World	90

MASS MEDIA AND COMMUNICATIONS

• the Church welcomes arrival of new forms of media	Communications	1
• the laity's role in shaping media for the Gospel	Communications	3
• use of media in education	Education	4
• place of media in shaping modern times	Modern World	6, 33, 51
• general reflections on media and ministry	Communications	1–24
• need for discretion in broadcasting Liturgy	Liturgy	20
• obligation of parents to reject what is evil	Communications	9

COLLEGIALITY AND THE OFFICE OF BISHOP

• power of the college of bishops defined	Church	21–23
• college of bishops responsible for entire world	Missionary Activity	38
• exercise of collegiate power of bishops	Bishops	1–10
• Synod of Bishops	Bishops	36–44
• bishops as successors of the apostles	Church	8, 18
• infallibility of the pope	Church	25
• apostolate of bishops	Church	21, 25
also:	Church in Modern World	43
	Bishops	11, 13, 16, 23
	Missionary Activity	38
	Life and Ministry of Priests	2

TOPIC	DOCUMENT	ARTICLE

ROMAN CURIA

• the place of the Curia in the Church and its need for reform	Bishops	9–10
• the specific curial office governing the spread of the Faith	Missionary Activity	29

NATURE OF MARRIAGE

• sacred nature of marriage and its place in life	Modern World	47–52
• married life as place where Christ dwells	Church	35
• marriage as an apostolate of the laity	Laity	11
• decision on number of children belongs to couple	Modern World	87
also:	Church	51
• spouses lead each other to holiness	Church	11, 41
• rights of parents defined	Laity	11
also:	Education	7–8

BAPTISM

• baptism into one Body	Church	7
• baptism and marriage	Church	11
• necessity of baptism	Church	14
• baptism and Paschal Mystery	Liturgy	6
• as the basis for unity	Ecumenism	3, 22
• a holy priesthood of baptized	Church	10
• the call to unity	Missionary Activity	6